12 BIRDS
BACK FROM THE BRINK

by Nancy Furstinger

12 STORY LIBRARY

www.12StoryLibrary.com

Copyright © 2015 by Peterson Publishing Company, North Mankato, MN 56003. All rights reserved. No part of this book may be reproduced or utilized in any form or by any means without written permission from the publisher.

12-Story Library is an imprint of Peterson Publishing Company and Press Room Editions.

Produced for 12-Story Library by Red Line Editorial

Photographs ©: Daniel Brigginshaw/Shutterstock Images, cover, 1, 7; Ricardo Arduengo/AP Images, 4; Floridastock/Shutterstock Images, 6; Janelle Lugg/Shutterstock Images, 8, 9, 29; John Flesher/AP Images, 10; Minden Pictures/SuperStock, 11; Connie Barr/Shutterstock Images, 12; critterbiz/Shutterstock Images, 13; Steve Byland/Shutterstock Images, 14, 28; Gerald Marella/Shutterstock Images, 15; Keneva Photography/Shutterstock Images, 16; Cliff Collings/Shutterstock Images, 17; kohihirano/Shutterstock Images, 18; George Lamson/Shutterstock Images, 19; feathercollector/Shutterstock Images, 20; US Fish and Wildlife Service/AP Images, 21; New Zealand Conservation Department/AP Images, 22; Igor Golovniov/Shutterstock Images, 23; Jack Jeffrey/US Geological Survey, 24; Caleb Slemmons, 25; Chris Hill/Shutterstock Images, 26; Teri Verbickis/Shutterstock Images, 27

ISBN
978-1-63235-001-5 (hardcover)
978-1-63235-061-9 (paperback)
978-1-62143-042-1 (hosted ebook)

Library of Congress Control Number: 2014937274

Printed in the United States of America
Mankato, MN
June, 2014

Go beyond the book. Get free, up-to-date content on this topic at 12StoryLibrary.com.

TABLE OF CONTENTS

COLORFUL PUERTO RICAN PARROTS SOAR ONCE AGAIN

Puerto Rican parrots have flashy colors. Their green feathers are tipped with blue. These parrots gather in flocks and squawk loudly. They nest in holes in tall trees. They search for food in the forest's canopy. But their numbers started to fall after humans came on the scene.

Puerto Rican parrots settled the main island of Puerto Rico long before people arrived. Approximately 1 million parrots lived on the island at the beginning of the 1500s. But over time, they began to face many dangers. People trapped the parrots. They sold them as pets and as food. Red-tailed hawks ate their eggs and chicks. Hurricanes blew down some of the

parrots' nesting trees. New trees became hard to find after people cut down forests for farms. Farmers planted citrus trees, coffee plants, and sugar cane. By 1975, only 13 Puerto Rican parrots were left in the wild.

Several government agencies in Puerto Rico and the United States worked together to start the Puerto

Puerto Rican parrots are the only parrots native to the United States.

IUCN RED LIST

The International Union for the Conservation of Nature (IUCN) keeps a list of all threatened species in the world, called the Red List. Each species is labeled according to how at risk it is.

Least Concern: Not considered at risk.

Near Threatened: At risk of being vulnerable or endangered in the future.

Vulnerable: At risk of extinction.

Endangered: At high risk of extinction.

Critically Endangered: At extremely high risk of extinction.

Extinct in the Wild: Only lives in captivity.

Extinct: No members of a species are left.

Rican Parrot Recovery Program. This program was launched in 1972 to help the parrots recover in the wild so they would no longer be endangered. Scientists collected eggs and chicks from the wild. They raised the parrots in aviaries. The first chick was born in 1979. It took scientists years to learn more about the birds and how to hatch them. The more scientists learned, the more successful they became. By 2013, almost 400 parrots were being raised in captivity.

Later, the scientists released some parrots in the Rio Abajo State Forest and El Yunque National Forest in Puerto Rico. The parrots started building nests in the forests and hatching chicks. By 2013, more than 100 birds could be tracked in the wild. Another 400 lived in captivity.

7
Number of years it took for the first chick to be born in captivity.

Status: Critically endangered
Population: Approximately 100 in the wild
Home: Puerto Rico
Life Span: Up to 50 years

BALD EAGLES MAKE A BIG COMEBACK

Bald eagles have wings that span up to eight feet (2.4 m). These large birds use their strong talons to fish. They also use them to snare prey, such as raccoons. Bald eagle pairs mate for life. They build huge stick nests where they tend to their eggs. But pesticides threatened the eagles' ability to hatch eggs.

A new pesticide called DDT started being used in 1939. People used it to kill insects that spread diseases or destroyed crops. But DDT also washed into lakes and rivers and poisoned the fish. Bald eagles ate the fish. The chemicals in DDT caused the eagles' eggs to have very thin shells. The shells broke open before the chicks were ready to hatch.

Once, hundreds of thousands of bald eagles soared across the United States. They became America's national bird in 1782. But by 1963, their numbers had fallen to 417 nesting pairs. They were listed as endangered in 1973. The Environmental Protection Agency banned DDT in 1972. The Clean Water Act was also passed

Bald eagles can most often be spotted near bodies of water.

The bald eagle is one of the largest raptor species.

in 1972. It limited the amount of pollution going into waterways where eagles fished.

As their food sources became safer, bald eagles made a comeback. In 2007, they were taken off the US Endangered Species List. At that time, more than 10,000 breeding pairs were nesting across the United States.

7,000
Number of feathers a bald eagle has.

Status: Least concern
Population:
  Approximately 10,000
  breeding pairs
Home: North America
Life Span: 15–30 years

KING PENGUIN NUMBERS ON THE RISE

King penguins get around by gliding through the water or sliding quickly on their bellies across the slick ice. Four layers of feathers keep them warm. During harsh winter storms, sometimes thousands of king penguins will huddle together for warmth. A mated pair will work hard to protect its egg from the cold.

The parents take turns balancing the egg on their feet. There the egg is warmed by their bellies. The chick hatches after 60 days.

King penguins live on islands north of the Antarctic. Hundreds of thousands of king penguins lived on Australia's Macquarie Island. People

Breeding colonies can range in size from dozens to thousands of king penguins.

King penguins are the second largest penguin species.

discovered this island in 1810. During the 1800s, hunters killed 3 million penguins for their blubber. This was used for lamp oil. Hunting was banned in 1919. By then, approximately 4,000 king penguins were left on the island.

In 1933, the island became a wildlife sanctuary where king penguins and other species were protected. Limits were also put on fishing to protect the penguins' food source. With these protections, the population of king penguins on Macquarie Island has grown to approximately 100,000 mating pairs.

1,125

Depth in feet (343 m) that a king penguin can dive to get fish and squid to eat.

Status: Least concern
Population: More than 2 million mating pairs, including 100,000 mating pairs on Macquarie Island
Home: Macquarie Island and other islands north of the Antarctic
Life Span: 15–20 years

THINK ABOUT IT

King penguins are thriving on many islands. Why do you think it was important to protect the species on Macquarie Island?

FOREST FIRES HELP KIRTLAND'S WARBLERS GROW

Kirtland's warblers only make their nests in young jack pine trees in and around Michigan. The trees have to be between six and 22 years old. Scientists think the age of the tree matters because warblers need low tree branches to hide their nests. Before six years, the low branches are not big enough. Later, they start falling off. Once this happens, the warblers have to move to younger trees. But jack pine trees will only open their cones and spread their seeds after a fire. When humans started controlling forest fires, new trees stopped growing. The warblers were running out of places to nest.

Kirtland's warblers are songbirds. Their call sounds like "chip-chip-che-way-oh."

9

Age in days at which the chicks first leave the nest.

Status: Near threatened
Population: More than 2,000 males
Home: Michigan, Wisconsin, and Ontario, Canada
Life Span: 5–7 years

Kirtland's warblers eat flying insects, grasses, and berries.

People used to think that fires were bad for a habitat. Later, scientists realized naturally occurring fires serve a purpose, such as clearing space for new trees to grow. Without fires, the warblers lost their nesting trees. Their population fell from more than 1,000 in 1961 to approximately 400 in 1971. They were listed as endangered in 1967.

Conservationists wanted the birds to return. They started managing the forest in the 1970s using controlled burns. In a controlled burn, a team of experts starts a fire and then carefully keeps it under control. The heat of these fires lets the pinecones open so the seeds will spread.

As new trees grew, the warblers started to nest again. People are now able to count the male warblers by their singing voices. The females are not counted because they do not sing. The number of males rose to more than 2,000 in 2012. The warblers also have started to spread to Wisconsin and Canada to nest.

WHOOPING CRANES BOUNCE BACK FROM NEAR EXTINCTION

Whooping cranes are the tallest birds in North America. They stand almost five feet (1.5 m) tall. These birds have long legs and necks. This helps them to forage for plants, fish, and frogs in shallow water. The cranes live in family groups. Baby cranes can walk and swim soon after they hatch. Whooping cranes nearly became extinct when people hunted them and drained their wetlands.

Whooping cranes nest in Canada and spend winters on the Gulf Coast of Texas. They have always been rare. Scientists think their population may never have been more than 20,000. The number fell dangerously low when people started hunting them in the 1800s. The whooping cranes also lost habitat when people filled in the marshes to grow crops. The number fell to approximately

When flying, a whooping crane stretches its long neck out in front of its body.

Whooping cranes are named for the loud "whooping" sounds they make.

MATING DANCE

Whooping cranes dance to attract mates. Both cranes dance side by side. They run and leap. They flap their giant wings and toss their heads. They even fling feathers and sticks. They sing a duet of loud calls. Each pair will stay together for life.

1,400 by 1860. In 1941, only 15 whooping cranes could be found.

Many groups are working hard to bring up the number of cranes. A wildlife research center in Maryland was the first to start breeding them in captivity in 1967. The young cranes are released in Wisconsin and given a new winter home in Florida. In 2001, the nonprofit organization Operation Migration started teaching the released birds to migrate. Pilots fly in ultra-light aircraft to lead the way. More than 500 whooping cranes flew from Wisconsin to their winter habitat in Florida in 2009.

90
Whooping crane's wingspan in inches (2.3 m).

Status: Endangered
Population: Approximately 500
Home: North America
Life Span: 22–24 years

13

NEST BOXES BRING BACK EASTERN BLUEBIRDS

Eastern bluebirds live east of the Rockies, from Canada to Mexico. They fly south in the winter and are one of the first birds to return north in the spring. After returning, the female half of a mating pair takes approximately 10 days to build a cup-shaped nest. When it's done, she lays one light blue egg each day until she has approximately four or five in the nest. After approximately two weeks, they hatch. Both parents feed the young birds insects until they are old enough to leave the nest. But other birds have forced bluebirds from their homes.

Bluebirds like to build their nests in old woodpecker holes. Birds such as house wrens battle them for control of these holes. House wrens are

The eastern bluebird is the state bird of Missouri and New York.

Eastern bluebirds perch on posts or branches in open spaces to scan for prey.

tiny but strong. They drag bluebird eggs and young out of nests. Then they take over. The bluebirds that once were a common sight almost disappeared by the mid-1950s.

In 1979, an article in *Parade* magazine pointed out ways to save the bluebird. It asked readers to send in a quarter to receive plans for building special nesting boxes. More than 80,000 readers responded. Many people built the nesting boxes. They were placed on fence posts in open spots. House wrens nest in wooded areas, so they did not bother to nest in the boxes. The eastern bluebirds thrived in their new homes. In 2012, the population was estimated at 22 million.

2
Notes that an eastern bluebird sings. It sounds like "too-lee."

Status: Least concern
Population: Approximately 22 million
Home: Eastern North America
Life Span: 6–10 years

15

BROWN PELICANS MAKE FULL RECOVERY

When they are fishing, brown pelicans plunge into the water. Then they scoop up fish into their throat pouch. This pouch hangs below the pelican's long beak and acts like a net. When it is full of water and fish, the pelican rises to the surface. It tips back the pouch to drain out the water, leaving behind the fish. In the 1950s, some of these fish turned out to be poisoned.

A brown pelican's beak can hold approximately three times as much as its stomach can.

3

Gallons (11 L) of water that the brown pelican's throat pouch can hold.

Status: Least concern
Population: Approximately 24,000
Home: North and South America
Life Span: 10–25 years

Brown pelicans have one of the longest bills of any bird. It measures 15–20 inches (38–51 cm).

Brown pelicans are the state bird of Louisiana. Thousands of the birds started dying in that state in the 1950s. Scientists found out a pesticide called Endrin had washed into rivers and the ocean. The fish in these waters were poisoned. Then pelicans ate the fish. The pesticide built up in the pelicans' bodies until they died.

The US government banned Endrin in 1986. Many pelicans had survived on Pelican Island off the Florida coast, where the pesticide had not reached. Some of these were sent to Louisiana between 1968 and 1980. They were last counted from helicopters in 2007. The count showed approximately 24,000— more than the state had in 1930, before Endrin was used.

SKY DIVERS

Brown pelicans can dive into the water from 65 feet (20 m) above. To protect themselves from the impact when they hit the water, they fill sacs under their skin with air. These cushions of air protect the pelicans' organs from harm.

CALIFORNIA CONDORS BACK TO SCAVENGING

California condors have no feathers on their heads. That is because these birds are scavengers. They eat dead animals, and bald heads help them to stay clean. They eat meat from the carcasses of large animals, such as deer or sheep. Sometimes, they will feed on smaller birds or rodents. But when humans developed the land the birds flew over, meals became harder to find.

California condors are the largest flying birds in North America. Their wings span up to 10 feet (3 m). These big birds need lots of space. They might travel 150 miles (241 km) every day to find a meal. Much of the open land that they soared over in California was developed into cities or farmland. Some condors also got lead

California condors can sometimes be spotted at Grand Canyon National Park.

poisoning when they fed on deer that had been killed by lead shotgun pellets.

In 1987, conservationists caught the last 22 condors in the wild. They bred them at zoos. In 1992, some of these birds began to be released in the wild. In 2011, a condor sanctuary on the coast of California provided the condors with 80 acres (32 ha) of space. Some deer hunters have switched to non-lead bullets to protect the condors' food supply. In 2013, the number of condors in the wild had risen to 435 worldwide. Of these, 237 condors were flying over California, Arizona, and Baja California, Mexico.

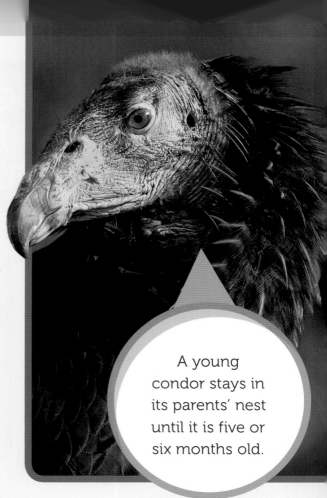

A young condor stays in its parents' nest until it is five or six months old.

15,000
Height in feet (4,572 m) that California condors can fly above land.

Status: Critically endangered
Population: 435 in the wild
Home: United States and Mexico
Life Span: Up to 60 years

PUPPET FEEDING

Zoo workers raised baby condors in breeding programs. The workers fed the baby birds with puppets that looked like bald condor heads. They did this so that the condors would bond with other condors, not people, before being released into the wild.

RED-COCKADED WOODPECKERS RETURN

Red-cockaded woodpeckers make their nests in live pine trees. They spend up to three years making nest holes. The birds flick layers of bark off the trees. Then they use their sharp beaks like chisels to chip a hole into the wood. Sticky sap drips out as the birds dig. This sap keeps snakes that climb trees away from the nests. Then loggers cut many of the pine trees down.

THINK ABOUT IT

Other species of birds like to use old woodpecker holes for nesting. How do you think these other birds were affected when the woodpeckers lost their habitat?

Red-cockaded woodpeckers make their nesting holes in aging pine trees because the decaying wood is softer.

The woodpeckers had fewer places to nest.

Loggers had been cutting down pine forests in the Southeast United States since approximately 1870. In 1970, the red-cockaded woodpeckers were listed as endangered. Conservation groups worked together to restore the woodpeckers' habitat. They planted new pine trees. Some of these trees were on private land or at military bases, while others were in national forests.

The new pine trees would take many years to grow. And it would take more years for the woodpeckers to dig out nest holes. So US wildlife officials gave the birds a head start. They made nest boxes and hammered these boxes into the trunks of small pine trees. Woodpeckers could start laying eggs in the nest boxes. In the first 10 years of the program, the population grew by 30 percent, to approximately 6,000. Since then, their numbers have risen to approximately 15,000.

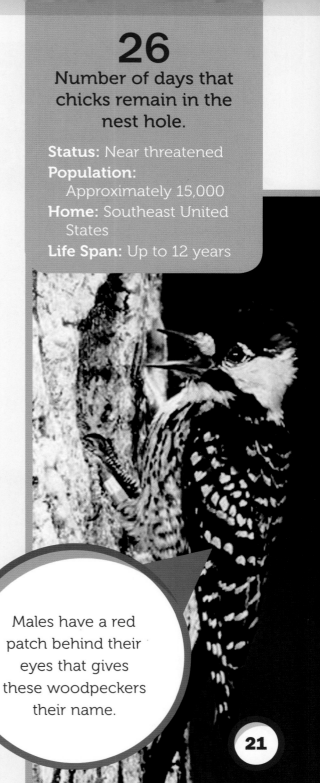

26
Number of days that chicks remain in the nest hole.

Status: Near threatened
Population:
    Approximately 15,000
Home: Southeast United
    States
Life Span: Up to 12 years

Males have a red patch behind their eyes that gives these woodpeckers their name.

KAKAPO PARROTS WADDLE BACK FROM EXTINCTION

Kakapo parrots are the only nocturnal parrots, meaning they are active at night. They are also the only parrot that doesn't fly. Kakapo parrots mostly live on two islands in New Zealand, where they did not have any natural predators. That changed when people arrived on the islands and brought other animals with them.

The first people to arrive thousands of years ago chopped down trees where the parrots lived. They hunted the parrots for food. They made cloaks out of the feathers. In the 1800s, European settlers arrived, bringing cats and rats with them. Because the Kakapo parrots nest on the ground and do not fly, the new animals caught them easily. In the

Kakapo parrots are sometimes called owl parrots or night parrots.

ON DISPLAY

Europeans sent a Kakapo skin back to England in the late 1800s to be studied. Many museums wanted this strange parrot on display. Hunters started killing more of the birds to sell to museums and private collectors. So many parrots had been shipped to England by the early 1930s that collectors no longer wanted them. The birds ended up being used in dog food.

early 1900s, the birds were thought to be extinct.

In the 1970s, small populations of Kakapo parrots were found on far-off islands. But rats and cats were starting to prey on the birds there, too. Conservationists trapped the birds and moved them to

islands without predators. They gave the birds extra food to help them lay eggs more often. The population has risen to approximately 127.

5

Number of islands where Kakapo parrots have been relocated since 1975.

Status: Critically endangered
Population: Approximately 127
Home: New Zealand
Life Span: More than 60 years

The Kakapo appeared on a New Zealand stamp to raise awareness of the species.

NEW ZEALAND

PALILAS NEST ON HAWAIIAN VOLCANO

Palilas, a kind of finch, can only be found on one volcano on Hawaii's Big Island. They live on the upper slopes of Mauna Kea, which has not erupted in 4,600 years. The palilas whistle a short song while they look for seeds of the Mamane tree and moth larvae. At dawn and dusk, their calls are louder and sharper. But new species brought to the island almost silenced the palilas' songs.

In the late 1700s, European farmers brought livestock to Hawaii.

Sheep and goats grazed on flowering plants that the birds depended on. Cats and rats ate palila eggs. Grasses planted by settlers stopped the Mamane tree, the palilas' main food source, from growing.

Palilas were listed as endangered in 1966. But little was done to save the birds until 1978. That's when an environmental group went to court to protect the birds. The court ruled that Hawaii had to prevent further damage to their habitat. The state

The palilas' song gets louder when rain is approaching.

A palila measures approximately six inches (15 cm) tall.

had to put up fences to keep livestock out of the palilas' habitat. The fences enclosed approximately 60,000 acres (24,000 ha) of land. Conservationists also caught some of the birds and released them on the other side of the volcano to try to expand their habitat. The first flock flew back. But many from the second flock stayed and started building nests.

12

Distance in miles (19 km) that the relocated flock flew home.

Status: Critically endangered
Population: 1,200
Home: Hawaii's Big Island
Life Span: Approximately 13 years

POISON SEEDS

Palilas live on the green seedpods of the Mamane tree. These seeds are very bitter. They are also poisonous. The seeds can kill a house finch within minutes. But palilas are able to eat the seeds without getting ill. One kind of caterpillar can also eat the seeds. The birds also eat these caterpillars.

PEREGRINE FALCONS BOUNCE BACK WITH BIGGER NUMBERS

Peregrine falcons fly faster than any other bird. They dive at speeds of more than 200 miles per hour (322 km/h). The falcons chase after smaller birds, such as pigeons. They catch the birds in mid-flight and kill them with a bite to the neck. But when their prey started to be poisoned, falcons' numbers took a nosedive.

In the mid-1900s, people used DDT on fields and marshes. This spray killed insects. When small birds ate the insects, the poison stayed in their bodies. Then falcons ate the small birds. The DDT built up in their bodies. It made the shells of their eggs very thin. The eggs cracked before they were ready to hatch. By the 1960s, few peregrine falcons were left in the United States.

The Peregrine Fund was started in 1970 to help the falcons. The fund helped

Peregrine falcons have a wingspan of more than three feet (0.9 m).

Peregrine falcons are known for their hooked beaks and sharp talons.

scientists to breed peregrine falcons in captivity to boost their numbers. The falcons lived in special chambers. They were fed vitamins to help the females lay strong eggs. The use of DDT was banned in 1972. After that, the young falcons could live in the wild again. Peregrine falcons were released around the United States. Their numbers climbed higher than they were before DDT came into use.

4,000

Number of falcons that the Peregrine Fund bred and released from 1974 to 1997.

Status: Least concern
Population: Approximately 3,000 nesting pairs in the United States
Home: All continents except Antarctica
Life Span: 17 years

THINK ABOUT IT

Birds of prey such as peregrine falcons are an important link in several food chains. They eat smaller birds, and other species eat the falcons' eggs. What do you think happens to the other species when this link is removed?

FACT SHEET

- While some bird species have made comebacks, many more are still in danger. The International Union for the Conservation of Nature lists 397 species of birds as endangered. Four others are extinct in the wild, and 198 are critically endangered.

- Many countries have laws protecting endangered animals. In 1973, the US Congress passed the Endangered Species Act. It requires state and federal government agencies to monitor and protect species that might become extinct. It also bans people from hunting, catching, trading, or possessing animals and plants that are protected.

- Pet cats kill an estimated 4 million birds every day in North America. Keeping pet cats indoors can limit this number.

- The two US federal agencies that deal with endangered species are the US Fish and Wildlife Service and the National Oceanic and Atmospheric Administration. Both have departments dedicated to identifying and helping endangered species.

- Several nonprofit organizations have been created to help threatened bird species. These nongovernmental groups include the American Bird Conservancy, the National Audubon Society, The Nature Conservancy, Partners in Flight, and the Royal Society for the Protection of Birds.

- Birds around the world have been affected by climate change. Warmer temperatures have caused habitat loss, especially near the North Pole and South Pole. Changing weather patterns have reduced birds' ability to reach their breeding grounds on time. Climate change could soon affect king penguins. When seas warm up, the penguins' food supply shrinks. Then these birds will have to travel greater distances to find the squid and lantern fish that they eat.

- Bald eagles are no longer considered an endangered species. But they remain protected under the Bald and Golden Eagle Protection Act and the Migratory Bird Treaty Act. These laws protect eagles, their nests, and their eggs.

- Bird lovers continue to help the bluebirds by keeping an eye on nest boxes. They visit the nests and record what they find. They take photos and videos of nesting birds. Some have even made roosting boxes where birds can keep warm in winter.

- The red-cockaded woodpeckers are the only woodpeckers to make homes in living trees. Other birds, such as screech owls, sometimes move into old nest holes. Raccoons, flying squirrels, bees, and wasps also claim the holes.

GLOSSARY

aviary
A protected place where birds are kept.

blubber
The fat of large sea mammals, such as whales.

breeding
The process by which animals or plants are produced by their parents.

canopy
Treetops in a forest that form a kind of ceiling.

conservationist
Someone who preserves, manages, and cares for the environment.

endangered
Threatened with extinction.

extinction
The death of all members of a species.

habitat
The place where a plant or animal naturally lives or grows.

migrate
To travel from one habitat to another.

pesticide
A chemical used to kill insect pests.

predator
An animal that kills or eats another animal.

prey
An animal that is killed or eaten by another animal.

sanctuary
A place where wildlife are protected from predators and people.

scavenger
An animal or bird that feeds on dead and rotting flesh.

threatened
At risk of becoming endangered.

FOR MORE INFORMATION

Books

Alderfer, Jonathan. *Bird Guide of North America*. Washington, DC: National Geographic Children's Books, 2013.

Boothroyd, Jennifer. *Endangered and Extinct Birds*. Minneapolis: Lerner, 2014.

George, Jean Craighead, and Wendell Minor. *The Eagles Are Back*. New York: Dial, 2013.

Haywood, Karen. *Hawks and Falcons*. Salt Lake City: Benchmark Books, 2010.

Roth, Susan L., and Cindy Trumbore. *Parrots over Puerto Rico*. New York: Lee & Low Books, 2013.

Websites

Discovery Kids: Birds
kids.discovery.com/tell-me/animals/birds

National Geographic Kids: Animals and Nature
kids.nationalgeographic.com/kids/stories/animalsnature

San Diego Zoo Kids: Birds
kids.sandiegozoo.org/animals/birds

US Fish & Wildlife Service: Endangered Species for Kids
www.fws.gov/endangered/education

INDEX

About the Author

Nancy Furstinger is the author of almost 100 books, including many on animals. She has been a feature writer for a daily newspaper, a managing editor of trade and consumer magazines, and an editor at two children's book publishing houses.

READ MORE FROM 12-STORY LIBRARY

Every 12-Story Library book is available in many formats, including Amazon Kindle and Apple iBooks. For more information, visit your device's store or 12StoryLibrary.com.

THE RISE OF APOCALYPSE

®: RISE OF APOCALYPSE ORIGINALLY PUBLISHED IN MAGAZINE FORM AS X-MEN®: RISE OF
LYPSE 'S 1-4, X-FACTOR 'S 5-6. PUBLISHED BY MARVEL COMICS, 387 PARK AVENUE SOUTH, NEW
N.Y. 10016. COPYRIGHT © 1986, 1996, 1998 MARVEL CHARACTERS, INC. ALL RIGHTS RESERVED.
(INCLUDING ALL PROMINENT CHARACTERS FEATURED IN THIS ISSUE AND THE DISTINCTIVE
ESSES THEREOF) IS A TRADEMARK OF MARVEL CHARACTERS, INC. NO PART OF THIS BOOK MAY BE
ED OR REPRODUCED IN ANY MANNER WITHOUT THE WRITTEN PERMISSION OF THE PUBLISHER.
ED IN THE U.S.A. FIRST PRINTING, FEBRUARY, 1998. ISBN 0-7851-0586-7. GST R127032852.
7 6 5 4 3 2

KARL BOLLERS
TEXT

JOHNNY GREENE
DESIGN

FRED HAYNES
SCOTT ELMER
DEREK MEI &
THOMAS VELAZQUEZ
COVER

ADDITIONAL MATERIAL BY
STAN LEE
JACK KIRBY &
DICK AYERS

MIKE HIGGINS
EDITOR

BOB HARRAS
EDITOR IN CHIEF

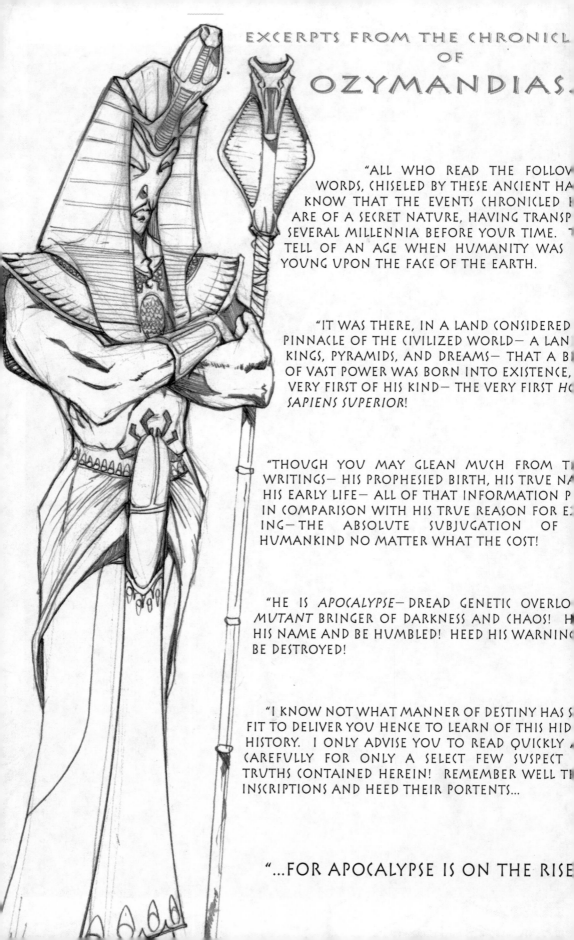

"ALL WHO READ THE FOLLOW
WORDS, CHISELED BY THESE ANCIENT HA
KNOW THAT THE EVENTS CHRONICLED I
ARE OF A SECRET NATURE, HAVING TRANSP
SEVERAL MILLENNIA BEFORE YOUR TIME. T
TELL OF AN AGE WHEN HUMANITY WAS
YOUNG UPON THE FACE OF THE EARTH.

"IT WAS THERE, IN A LAND CONSIDERED
PINNACLE OF THE CIVILIZED WORLD— A LAN
KINGS, PYRAMIDS, AND DREAMS— THAT A BI
OF VAST POWER WAS BORN INTO EXISTENCE,
VERY FIRST OF HIS KIND— THE VERY FIRST HO
SAPIENS SUPERIOR!

"THOUGH YOU MAY GLEAN MUCH FROM TI
WRITINGS— HIS PROPHESIED BIRTH, HIS TRUE NA
HIS EARLY LIFE— ALL OF THAT INFORMATION P
IN COMPARISON WITH HIS TRUE REASON FOR E:
ING— THE ABSOLUTE SUBJUGATION OF
HUMANKIND NO MATTER WHAT THE COST!

"HE IS *APOCALYPSE*— DREAD GENETIC OVERLO
MUTANT BRINGER OF DARKNESS AND CHAOS! H
HIS NAME AND BE HUMBLED! HEED HIS WARNIN(
BE DESTROYED!

"I KNOW NOT WHAT MANNER OF DESTINY HAS S
FIT TO DELIVER YOU HENCE TO LEARN OF THIS HID
HISTORY. I ONLY ADVISE YOU TO READ QUICKLY A
CAREFULLY FOR ONLY A SELECT FEW SUSPECT
TRUTHS CONTAINED HEREIN! REMEMBER WELL TI
INSCRIPTIONS AND HEED THEIR PORTENTS...

"...FOR APOCALYPSE IS ON THE RISE

Stan Lee PRESENTS:

HAMMER & CHISEL

TERRY KAVANAGH
WRITER
ADAM POLLINA
PENCILER
MARK MORALES
& HARRY CANDELARIO
INKERS
RICHARD STARKINGS
& COMICRAFT
LETTERS
CHRIS LICHTNER
COLORIST
MALIBU
ENHANCEMENT
MARK POWERS
EDITOR
AND BOB HARRAS
EDITOR-IN-CHIEF
BRING YOU...

-- THE ORIGIN OF THE X-MEN'S GREATEST FOE

WITHIN THE SUDDENLY WHIRLING WINDS OF BLINDING SILT AND SEDIMENT --

AAIEEEE!

-- COME THE SANDSTORMERS.

RAIDERS AND SCAVENGERS UNMATCHED IN ANY AGE, ANY LAND.

THE PEOPLE OF THE STORM ARE FAR AND AWAY THE MOST FEARED AND FURIOUS TRIBE OF THEIR TIME.

...SSES...

...NEARLY TWO DECADES, TO BE PRECISE.

...TY OF THE MYSTERIOUS ...AOH, RAMA-TUT, A CITY ...ONDROUS MARVELS ...D SECRET TERRORS.

...THOSE WHO ENTER ITS MASSIVE GATES TREMBLE BEFORE THE ...OWER OF A KING WHO APPEARED FROM THE HEAVENS AND ...SUBJUGATED ALL OF EGYPT.

INSIDE HIS PALACE, THE HEART OF HIS EMPIRE, WHERE ONLY HIS MOST TRUSTED AIDES DARE TREAD......

STAND ASIDE, OZYMANDIAS! I HAVE NEWS OF GREAT IMPORT FOR THE PHARAOH --

WHAT NEWS COULD A SCHOLAR LIKE YOU POSSIBLY HAVE THAT WOULD BE OF ANY INTEREST TO A CONQUEROR, LOGOS? COME BACK LATER AND TELL HIM OF YOUR FOOL THEORIES ABOUT THE MOON AND THE SUN...

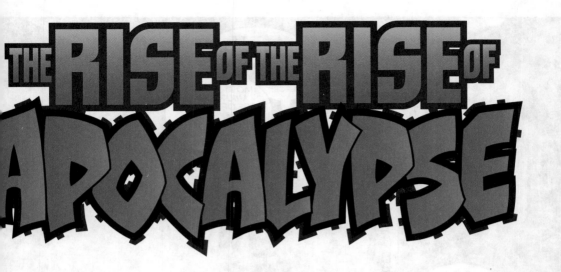

X-FACTORY MADE...

1985: The editorial offices of Marvel Comics, where neophyte
r Mike Carlin was eagerly toiling away with his trustworthy
tant Mike Higgins, toward the launch of a new ongoing comic
series that would reunite the original members of the popu-
per hero team title, THE UNCANNY X-MEN. The heroes to be
red were Cyclops, Marvel Girl, Beast, Angel, and Iceman, who
been 'ousted' from the pages of their book by the introduction
new, more multicultural roster of galaxy-protecting mutants
h gained an increasing popularity amongst fandom. This
ense reader response spurred the execs at Marvel to push for
-pansion' of the entire line of mutant comics, and when X-
'OR debuted with the creative team of Bob Layton and
son Guice it wasn't long before it was sharing the success of
ster title. But now that the book was off and running, how
d it maintain its reputation and not simply seem like an
ANNY X-MEN imitation? The comic was in need of some-
. But what exactly was that something? New stories? New
ns? What?

-- FOR THE *UNBELIEVABLE*.

WH -- WHAT *IS* THIS PLACE?

A MOST WICKED *MIRACLE*. A PLACE OF WONDERS AND *MYSTERIES* PERTAINING TO THE PHARAOH.

THE *PHARAOH* --?! FATHER, WE SHOULD NOT *BE* HERE!

THIS IS A DWELLING PLACE FOR THE *DIVINE*! WHAT IF *RAMA-TUT* SENSES OUR PRESENCE?

PLEASE, SON. DO NOT FALL VICTIM TO THE MISCONCEPTIONS OF THE *IGNORANT*.

RAMA-TUT IS *NO* GOD.

HE IS A *MAN*. A *MYSTERIOUS* MAN, BUT ONE NONETHE-LESS.

RRR

MADE OF HIM A *SURVIVOR*... MUCH AS I WOULD DO FOR YOU, SOON AFTER.

BUT THE ACCURSED STRANGER *BETRAYED* US, AND WITH HIS IMPOSSIBLE WEAPONS WE COULD NOT BEGIN TO UNDER-STAND...

... *ENSLAVED* THE CLAN.

HE *TORTURED* US TO BRING HIM BACK HERE, BUT WE WERE *STRONG* -- AND *NONE* EVER REVEALED THIS LOCATION TO HIM.

A TRAGIC FEW *ESCAPED*, AND HE HAS HUNTED US ALL LIKE ANIMALS EVER SINCE.

TH... WHAT I... THAT IMPOR... TO H...

FLY LIKE AN OWL...

1986: X-FACTOR continued strongly, maintaining its position as
top-selling comic. But never content to rest on its laurels, Marvel still felt
the team needed something to distinguish itself from the X-Men in term
its approach to making the world a better place for humans and mutant
peacefully coexist.

It was decided that the misfit mutant team was in need of a major
lain to round out the dynamics of the fledgling title. The Editor in Chief
wanted to spotlight the Owl, feeling that this classic character had never
ly had his moment in the sun. Having made his debut in DAREDEVIL, THE M
WITHOUT FEAR, the Owl had already been established as a heavy, but
that was capable of going toe-to-toe with only non-superpowered champi
The idea was part of a scheme to revamp the Owl, at last presenting him
foe capable of holding his own against such staples of the pantheon of Ma
heroes as the Fantastic Four and the
Avengers... or in this case, X-Factor.

However, these designs never
came to fruition because later that year,
when X-FACTOR's editorial and creative
team departed to undertake other assignments
in the comics field, the book's direction was left
up in the air, so to speak.

Shown here is art from X-FACTOR #5. The shadowy figure was originally draw
the Owl. A few quick art corrections and some additions to his gauntlets, and
book's direction changed its creative course— a new villain was on the rise!

FIVE MILLENNIA AGO...

IT IS A TIME OF GREAT CHANGE.

IN THE CRADLE OF THE NILE -- THE MYSTICAL LAND CALLED EGYPT -- THE HUMAN RACE CRAWLS TOWARD CIVILIZATION.

OUTSIDE THE GOLDEN CITY, NOMADS RULE BY SAVAGERY, MARKING TERRITORY WITH SWORD AND SPEAR.

IT WAS DURING THIS EPOCH THAT A SINGLE MAN WAS BORN...

...ONE WHO WOULD OUTLIVE THESE PYRAMIDS, THESE MONUMENTS MEANT TO OUTLAST TIME ITSELF, TO BECOME HISTORY'S MOST NOTORIOUS VILLAIN --

-- THE GENETIC OVERLORD KNOWN AS APOCALYPSE!

THIS IS THE TALE OF HOW HE CAME TO BE.

THE DESERT IS RULED BY THREE FORCES.

THE BARREN WASTELANDS ARE PREYED UPON BY THE FIERCE TRIBE OF THE SANDSTORMERS...

WHILE THE FERTILE NILE-BOUND SOCIETY IS CONTROLLED BY THE IRON HEEL OF THE MYSTERIOUS PHARAOH RAMA-TUT AND HIS POWER-MAD WARLORD, OZYMANDIAS.

OVER THEM ALL, THERE IS THE SMITING, SKIN-BLISTERING FURY OF NATURE.

...HOURS AGO, THE FORCES OF EGYPT AND THE SANDSTORMERS CLASHED TO THE DEATH...

...ONLY TO BE BURIED TOGETHER BY A MASSIVE CAVE-IN.

Stan Lee
PRESENTS:

BLOOD OF THE FATHER

TERRY KAVANAGH
WITH JAMES FELDER
WRITER
ADAM POLLINA
PENCILER
MARK MORALES
INKER
RICHARD STARKINGS
& COMICRAFT
LETTERS
CHRIS LICHTNER
COLORIST
JENNIFER SCHELLINGER
& CO.
ENHANCEMENT
MARK POWERS
EDITOR
AND BOB HARRAS
EDITOR IN CHIEF
BRING YOU...

...THE ORIGIN OF THE
X-MEN'S GREATEST
FOE!

THE CAMP OF THE
SANDSTORMERS IS NOW A CITY
OF THE DEAD.

ALL LIE LIF
FROM
MASSAC

...SAVE ONE.

LET THE GODS HURL
THE DESERT AT
ME, LET THE EARTH
TRY TO BURY ME
IN ITS MASSY
GRIP.

I AM
THE GLORY
OF EGYPT, I AM
THE RIGHTFUL
KING --

-- AND TUT
CANNOT BE
RID OF ME SO
EASILY!

LET
THE GODS
COME, FOR
I AM...

...OZYMANDIAS

AND LET MANKI
TREMBLE AT
ANGER...

THE
RS PASS
NOW, AT
E END.

THE
EDING IS
OPPED.

THE
BROKEN
BONES
SET.

YOU SHOULD NOT BE ALIVE AND YET YOU *ARE*...

PERHAPS THERE IS A *HOPE*.

WE HAVE ALWAYS LIVED IN THE TRIBE BY *SURVIVAL OF THE FITTEST*...

...IT IS THE ONLY THING THAT KEPT US FROM *OBLIVION* IN THIS HARSH WORLD.

AND NOW IT CLAIMS US BOTH IF I CAN'T GET YOU *OUT* OF HERE.

IN THIS TOMB, FAR GREATER AND *FEARSOME* THAN THE PYRAMIDS OF THE PHARAOH'S, THE HOPES OF THE PEOPLE OF THE SANDS MAY *DIE*.

THEN PHARAOH RAMA-TUT WILL *SUCCEED* AND TRULY BE LIKE UNTO A GOD --

-- FOR HE SHALL HAVE CRUSHED US TO *DUST* AND *SCATTERED* US BACK TO THE SANDS WE CAME FROM.

THIS CAN'T BE *ALLOWED*.

IT *WON'T* BE.

EVEN NOW, SIRE, I FEEL A *STIRRING* INSIDE ME.

I HAVE SEEN THE *CRYPTIC VISIONS* OF THE *EYE OF THE AGES*.

NO MORE SHALL I BE *WHIPPED* AND *HUNTED*.

WE WILL NO LONGER HAVE TO RUN, *FATHER*, WE SHALL *RULE*.

AND PHARAOH WILL *TREMBLE*. ONLY THE *FIT* WILL SURVIVE MY ARRIVAL.

THIS I *SWEAR*!

I WILL BE THE *TEST* UNTO TUT'S KINGDOM.

OZYMANDIAS.

BELOVED. REVERED. BUT MOST OF ALL...

...FEARED BY HIS PEOPLE.

THE GOD ON EARTH THAT IS THE PHARAOH, RULES THIS LONE BASTION OF SOCIETY ON THE LUSH BANKS OF THE NILE.

HERE STAND THE TALLEST MONUMENTS EVER ERECTED BY MAN.

HERE EXIST THE GREATEST ENGINEERING FEATS IN HISTORY...

HERE THE DA[Y] COURSE OF THE IS CHARTED BY VIZIER, LOGOS, HIS STRANGE CALLED SCIEN[CE]

HE HAS MADE THE CORNERS OF THE KNOWN WORLD RUN RIVERS OF BLOOD AND BOW TO THE MIGHTY WARLORD.

HE RETURNS HOME FROM THE CAMPAIGN IN THE DESERT ON AN AUSPICIOUS DAY AT THE CENTER OF THE CIVILIZED WORLD -- THE FESTIVAL OF THE SCARAB.

A TIME OF OMENS AND CHANGE IN PHARAOH'S DOMAIN.

...LACE FIT ...ODS --

-- BUT GIVEN TO MAN BY THE OUTLANDER KNOWN ONLY AS RAMA-TUT.

...NDERER-KING ...APPEARED ...ULOUSLY TO THE THRONE...

...SUBDUE ...LAND.

BEHOLD THE SPLENDOR THAT IS --

-- THE CITY OF KINGS!

"-- A *PORTENT* OF THE GODS COMING BACK TO RULE.

THE *SPHINX*, GUARDIAN OF EGYPT, THEY SAY FELL FROM THE SKY --

"A *WEAK-MINDED* NOTION.

"I *SAW* THAT VESSEL FALL TO EARTH...

"... AND ONLY *OUR* PEOPLE SAW THE BURNING FRAGMENT THAT *BROKE* FROM IT.

"INSIDE THE JEWEL WAS A *MAN* GARBED WEIRD AND *WONDROUS*.

"BROKEN AND *BLIND*, WE BROUGHT HIM BACK TO OUR CAMP.

"YOU MUST BE ABLE TO RECOGNIZE WHEN SOMETHING POWERFUL APPROACHES ON THE HORIZON, BOY. SURVIVAL *DEPENDS* ON THIS.

"FOR WEEKS WE TENDED TO HIS WOUNDS -- HE WOULD HAVE *DIED* IF NOT FOR OUR CHARITY.

"THIS MAN... THIS *TRAVELER*... I NAMED RAMA-TUT --

"--'THE VISTOR FROM BEYOND THE SUN.'"

"ONE MORNING, WE AWAKENED TO FIND HE HAD WANDERED AWAY DURING THE NIGHT, TAKING WITH HIM THE STRANGE *OBJECTS* WE HAD FOUND IN HIS VESSEL..."

"... HIS FOOTSTEPS FADING TOWARD THE PHARAOH'S LANDS.

"WEEKS LATER, HE RETURNED, HIS SIGHT *RESTORED*, WIELDING STRANGE WEAPONRY AND *COMMANDING* EGYPT'S ARMY.

"TUT DEMANDED TO KNOW WHERE HIS JEWEL LAY.

"THIS WE *NEVER* REVEALED TO HIM...

"... EVEN WHEN HE *MASSACRED* OUR PEOPLE AND *ENSLAVED* MOST OF THE SURVIVORS.

"HE THOUGHT US CRUSHED, BUT I HAD FOUND THE *EYE OF THE AGES*...

"... AND IN IT I SAW THE FACE OF A MAN POWERFUL ENOUGH TO *DEFEAT* HIM.

"A MAN LOOK[ING] OVER THOUSA[NDS] OF WORSHIPE[RS,] THE RULER O[F] ALL THE WORL[D.]

WHATEVER PLACE TUT HAD *COME* FROM, HE KNEW OF YOU...

... AND HE WILL USE ALL THE POWER OF HIS KINGDOM TO *TAKE* YOU.

IT WAS *YOU,* EN SABAH NUR!

THE CITY OF KINGS. WORK HAS CONTINUED UNSTOPPED ON THE PYRAMIDS FOR DECADES --

-- THROUGH HOT DAYS INTO COLD NIGHTS.

THESE ENGINEERING MARVELS RISE HIGH INTO THE DESERT SKY, THEIR ONLY MORTAR BEING THE BLOOD OF SLAVES.

HERE THE MIGHTY WARLORD OF EGYPT OVERSEES THE PHARAOH'S WORK IN THESE UNFORTUNATE PERIODS OF PEACE.

SSNKKACS

BAH! THIS IS A POOR SUBSTITUTE FOR THE SWORD.

I WOULD MAKE WAR ON THE GODS, JUST AS AN EXCUSE TO PUT THIS FLACCID WHIP DOWN.

Soon.

LOOK -- ABOUT US ARE SIGNS OF HOW SPECIAL YOU ARE, OF THE GLORY THAT AWAITS YOU.

READ FROM THESE HIEROGLYPHS, AS I DID YEARS AGO.

"...FROM THE SANDS HE COMES. NEITHER GOD NOR MAN..."

"...KINGDOMS BOW AT HIS FEET AND MANKIND WEEPS IN HIS PRESENCE..."

"...HE IS EN SABAH NUR... THE FIRST ONE."

YOU ARE TO BE MY WEAPON AGAINST PHARAOH -- MY HOPE FOR TOMORROW!

YOU KEEP TELLING ME OF GRAND DESTINIES AND PROPHECY CARVED IN STONE.

LOOK AT ME! NOT WITH THE EYES OF A PARENT, BUT WITH THOSE OF A STRANGER!

WHAT CRUEL JO HAS NATI PLAYED HERE?

WHY WAS I BORN L THIS?

BUT DID YOU EVER CONSIDER, FATHER, THAT WHATEVER PERSON ALL YOUR SIGNS AND PORTENTS SPEAK OF --

-- MIGHT NOT BE YOUR SON?

TEARS. I HAVE NOT CRIED SINCE MY FATHER DIED. CAN IT BE --

-- TEARS OF *HOPE?*

WHO IS THIS STRANGER LOGOS SPEAKS TO -- DOES HE DARE OPPOSE BOTH TUT *AND* MY BROTHER?

IS THERE *TRULY* HOPE FOR ME, FOR *MOTHER* EGYPT?

I CARE NOT FOR THIS *CIVILIZATION* OF YOURS... I HAVE ONLY SEEN IT TO BE *CRUEL* AND *CAPRICIOUS.*

NOR DO I LIKE *HIDING* MYSELF UNDER A SLAVE'S WRAPPINGS.

ALL I WANT ARE THE HEADS OF RAMA-TUT AND HIS GENERAL.

ONE LAST HOPE FOR *ME...*

COME, DEAR

... YOU HAVE YOUR PHARAOH TO SERVE.

I AM NOT THE ONLY ONE WHO SEES THE MADNESS AFOOT HERE -- I AM NOT ALONE -- HE IS A KINDRED SPIRIT.

I WILL HAVE WORDS WITH HIM.

MAY *ISIS* WATCH OVER YOU, MY BOLD *STRANGER...*

WHAT IS THIS? *WARM RAIN?*

A GIRL UP THERE... *CRYING?*

WHO *IS* SHE, LOGOS?

HOW CAN I GET TO SEE HER?

SO MUCH BEAUTY AND UGLINESS IN ONE PLACE --

-- THIS TRULY IS A PLACE OF *WONDER.*

AND IT SHALL BE *MINE!*

**[NEXT:] EGYPT AFLAME!
APOCALYPSE'S
FURY UNBOUND!**

HE MOVES THE MASSIVE STONE *SINGLE-HANDEDLY.*

HIS STRENGTH IS *UNGODLY...*

STAN LEE
PRESENTS:

THE FACE OF THE GODS

TERRY KAVANAGH
AND JAMES FELDER
WRITERS

ADAM POLLINA
PENCILER

MARK MORALES
INKER

RICHARD STARKINGS
& COMICRAFT
LETTERS

CHRISTIAN LICHTNER
COLORIST

GRAPHICS
COLORWORKS
SEPARATIONS

MARK
POWERS
EDITOR

BOBA TUT
HARRAS
CHIEF

... THE ORIGIN OF THE X-MEN'S GREATEST FOE!

THEY WILL HAVE NO MONUMENTS ERECTED BY SLAVES TO MARK THEIR PASSING, ONLY NUR'S MEMORY...

... WHICH WILL OUTLAST EVEN THESE SENTINELS MEANT TO OVERWATCH ETERNITY.

YOU HAVE TAKEN EVERYTHING FROM ME -- MY *HOME...*

...AND BAAL, WH PROTECT ME LIKE *FATHER*

...AND IT INSPIRES *FEAR* IN SLAVE AND MASTER ALIKE.

"HE CANNOT BE *HUMAN*," THEY WHISPER.

BUT NUR IS USED TO BEING AN OUTCAST.

HE HAD BEEN *ABANDONED* IN THE WASTES TO DIE AS A FREAKISH BABE...

...AND THEN SHUNNED BY THE TRIBE -- THE *PEOPLE OF THE SANDS* --

-- THAT TOOK HIM IN UPON THE INSISTENCE OF THEIR LEADER, *BAAL.*

HIS TWISTED FEATURES ARE SWATHED IN RAGS TO DISGUISE HIM.

FOR IN THIS CITY OF HIDDEN MENACE, HE IS *HUNTED* BY EGYPT'S MYSTERIOUS RULER, *RAMA-TUT*...

...WHO WANTS THE YOUTH'S BURGEONING POWER FOR HIS OWN USE.

ALREADY, NUR'S TRIBE LIES DEAD BECAUSE OF PHARAOH'S WARLORD, *OZYMANDIAS.*

SOON...

...SOON I WILL HAVE MY REVENGE UPON YOU AND YOUR GENERAL BOTH, TUT.

AND THEN I WILL CLAIM THE SECRETS MY FATHER SPOKE OF THAT LIE WITHIN YOUR PRECIOUS SPHINX.

TAKE THEM AWAY TO AWAIT MY PLEASURE.

BUT *YOU* SHALL REMAIN AT MY SIDE!

FOR YOU HAVE TRAVELED ALL THESE CENTURIES BACK THROUGH TIME... AND YOU SHALL BE REWARDED...

... BY BECOMING MY *QUEEN!*

IN LOGOS' BARREN CHAMBER...

THIS IS MY REWARD FOR SERVING *EGYPT?*

MY PLANS AND SCHEMATICS FOR THE PYRAMIDS *SEIZED* BY OZYMANDIAS' MEN.

NOW THE GENERAL READIES HIMSELF TO *TAKE* THE THRONE...

... WHILE TUT ALLIES HIMSELF WITH MORE OUTLANDERS WITH UNIMAGINABLE POWERS.

NOT EVEN OZYMANDIAS' *SAVAGERY* CAN *STOP* THEM!

I MUST ACT *SOON* -- OR I WILL DIE, AND EGYPT WILL BE *DESTROYED.*

MY ONLY HO IS EN SA NUR.

WHERE ARE YOU WHI I *NEED* YO BOY?

JUST THIS SIDE OF THE UNDERWORLD...

UHH... WHERE AM I? WHAT HAS HAPPENED?

HUSH. *REST.*

YOU ARE DEEP WITHIN THE BURIAL CHAMBER OF RAMA-TUT -- WITHIN THE *MAIN PYRAMID.*

HERE YOU CAN *HIDE* AND REGAIN YOUR STRENGTH.

WHO ARE YOU..?

I AM *NEPHRI* -- PROMISED TO WED PHARAOH.

THIS HAS GIVEN ME FREE PASSAGE OF THE GROUNDS -- EVEN SOME SECRET PASSAGES.

INTO *HERE...* ONTO THE *SLAVE FIELDS...* EVEN CLOSE TO THE *SPHINX* --

WHAT?!

SUDDENLY...

PHARAOH! WHY HAS WORK STOPPED ON THE PYRAMIDS?

FIRST, THE EQUIPMENT IN MY LAB WAS *SEIZED*. NOW I AM DENIED ACCESS TO THE *PYRAMID GROUNDS*.

I --

-- THE WOMAN IN THE GARB OF *PHARAOH'S BETROTHED?* TUT PICKS ANOTHER *FOREIGNER* TO BE HIS BRIDE? BUT THEN, WHAT OF *NEPHRI?*

DO NOT TROUBLE YOURSELF WITH THOSE TOMBS. OZYMANDIAS ALERTED US TO A PROBLEM -- -- THE WORKERS HAD TO BE *DISPOSED* OF.

THEY THREATENED *REVOLT* BECAUSE OF SOME HEATHEN *SAVIOR* THEY THOUGHT HAD ARRIVED.

A DISGUISED STRANGER AMONGST THEM WHO SEEMED TO PERFORM... *MIRACLES.*

I AM IN AS MUCH IGNORANCE OF THIS MATTER AS *YOU* ARE, WISE LOGOS.

WE ALL SEEK ANSWERS -- LIVES HANG IN THE BALANCE, *NO?*

I AM TOLD YOU HAD A SLAVE WITH BANDAGED FACE IN *YOUR* QUARTERS EARLIER.

ANSWE.. ME, MY TRUSTE.. VIZIER.

MEANWHILE...

GO BACK NOW. YOU'VE SHOWN ME PASSAGE -- BEYOND HERE LIES MY DESTINY.

THIS IS A PLACE OF EVIL!

THE SPHINX IS SAID TO HAVE APPEARED FROM NOWHERE...

...WITH TUT HIMSELF!

MORE TALK OF OMENS, NEPHRI?

DO NOT MOCK ME!

THE SPHINX DOES NOT GUARD OVER MY EGYPT, BUT OVER PHARAOH'S WORLD --

-- IT STANDS READY TO DEVOUR THOSE WHO SEEK THE SECRETS OF THE KING!

DON'T TAKE THAT TONE.

I'M AN OUTLANDER. MORE SO THAN ANY...

...AND THOSE SECRETS WILL BE MINE, NEPHRI.

RETURN TO YOUR LIFE IN THE PALACE...

...WHERE IT'S SAFE. MY PLACE IS HERE --

-- ALONE, AS I ALWAYS HAVE BEEN.

I WILL NOT LEAVE YOU. YOU CANNOT DISMISS ME!

THIS LAND NEEDS YOUR POWER -- YOUR COURAGE!

EVEN IF YOU DO NOT WANT ME TO --

I... DO WANT YOU HERE.

BUT I WOULDN'T SEE YOU HURT.

ALREADY ONE PERSON DIED THAT I... ...THAT I SHOULD HAVE PROTECTED.

NEPHRI, I DON'T HAVE THE WORDS TO SAY THIS...

...BUT I'M NOT FROM YOUR COURT OF LEARNING AND CULTURE.

I'M JUST A NOMAD SEEKING TO PROTECT YOU FROM WHAT LIES...

...WITHIN.

BY THE BURNING SANDS!

SOON...

Stan Lee PRESENTS:

THE CONCLUSION TO THE ORIGIN OF APOCALYPSE

THE FIRST CULLING

TERRY KAVANAGH AND JAMES FELDER
WRITERS

ADAM POLLINA & ANTHONY WILLIAMS
PENCILER

MARK MORALES & AL MILGROM
INKER

RICHARD STARKINGS & COMICRAFT
LETTERS

CHRISTIAN LICHTNER
COLORIST

GRAPHICS COLORWORKS
SEPARATIONS

MARK POWERS
EDITOR

BOBA TUT

HARRAS
CHIEF

HERE IS WHERE THE WORKER RABBLE ARE CAST OFF WHEN THEY DIE...

...SO THAT WE MIGHT HAVE COMPOST FOR THE DELTA FIELDS.

YOUR F-FACE... GET AWAY FROM ME! GET AWAY!

DON'T, NEPHRI. DON'T..!

HERE, SISTER --

-- WE WILL PROTECT YOU.

KILL HIM...

NEPHRI...

THEY DISMISS HIM AS AN ANIMAL.

THE COMFORTS OF THESE "CIVILIZED" PEOPLE -- HAPPINESS... LOVE -- CAN HAVE NO MEANING FOR HIM AFTER THIS LAST BETRAYAL.

ONCE HE WOULD HAVE SACRIFICED HIS LIFE FOR THIS... FOR ONE WOMAN.

NO MORE.

EVERY BRUTAL LESSON HE LEARNED FROM THE DESERT NOMADS HAS BEEN PROVEN IN THESE ROYAL COURTS...

... FOR THE WAY OF LIFE HERE IS NO LESS FIERCE THAN IN THE WILD.

HE HAS TURNED HIS BACK ON THIS TWO-FACED THING CALLED HUMANITY FOR ALL ETERNITY --

-- THERE IS O SURVIVAL NO THE TEST OF LI

THE WEAK PERISH...

...AND STRONG SURVI

WHO GIVES A HOOT..?

The new editor of X-FACTOR had a tough task ahead of him, not to
on having some pretty big shoes to fill. It was his job to keep the cre-
parks flying on the title and to maintain the success that had become
mark. His name was Bob Harras and he knew one thing— the Owl was
eant to be—in any way, shape, or fashion—part of his scheme for the
Harras, feeling that the team needed to face a new villain who would
within the pages of that title, rather than an old villain looking for refur-
ent, enlisted the talented Louise Simonson to help him plot a new

Simonson, the new writer, had an extensive amount of experience with
enetic nomenclature known as mutants, having been the editor of THE
NNY X-MEN for several years. Together with Harras, she and Guice
had stayed on as penciler) set about the creation of a new ne'er-do-well.
weeks of brainstorming story ideas with Simonson and countless char-
sketches from Guice's art table, the Owl's replacement came forth. It
villain sure to shake the Marvel Universe to its very foundations.!
me— APOCALYPSE!

What Bob, Louise, and Jackson weren't prepared for was the enormous
sponse to the character's introduction. Apocalypse went on to become
or villain throughout the X-Men titles, establishing himself as a menace
Marvel Universe not only in its past and present, but in its future as

WHAT THE PEOPLE SEE IS FRIGHTENING ENOUGH --

-- BUT WHAT EN SABAH NUR HAS EXPERIENCED IS WORSE.

THE BOY HAS JUST DISCOVERED HIS GENETIC POWER TO CAST OFF HIS HUMAN FORM AND REMAKE IT --

-- AND WHAT TERRIBLE FORM IT SHALL ASSUME.

THIS IS WHAT TUT KNEW WOULD HAPPEN... HE IS UNEARTHLY!

WHERE HAS PHARAOH GONE? HE HAS ABANDONED US AND THE KINGDOM IS LOST!

WHO SHALL LEAD US? THE GODS RUN AMOK IN THE CITY OF THE KINGS!

TONIGHT, I START DOWN MY OWN PATH.

MONSTERS ARE MEANT TO BE SLAIN SO HEROES MAY BE CROWNED, NUR.

YOU SHALL BE MY WAY INTO THE SPHINX...

TUT GUARDED CLOSELY WHAT LAY HIDDEN WITHIN THE SPHINX. ALL SECRETS ARE MINE, NOW. ALL GATES LIE OPEN. NEVER AGAIN SHALL MY WAY LIE BARRED!

... AND YOUR CORPSE ON MY SWORD WILL BE MY KEY TO THE OPAL THRONE.

AND AS OZYMANDIAS PASSES OUT, REELING UNDER THE SECRET KNOWLEDGE THAT HE SO DESPERATELY DESIRED...

...HE REALIZES -- SEEING WHAT IS TO COME OVER THE CENTURIES FOR A SPLIT SECOND BEFORE IT EXPLODES FROM HIS MEMORY --

--THAT HE WILL BE ONLY THE FIRST TO BE TRANSFORMED AND DAMNED BY THE RAGE OF APOCALYPSE.

WHILE NUR UNLEASHES HIS RAGE ON PHARAOH'S TECHNOLOGY...

...TUT RETURNS TO HIS FUTURE IN HIS TIME CAPSULE, REPULSED BY THE COMBINED FORCES OF THOSE ADVENTURERS FROM THE TWENTIETH CENTURY --

-- THE FANTASTIC FOUR!

BWOOORRMM

OMENS! OMENS!

FIRE IN THE SKY!

OUR ERSTWHILE TEAM MAKES THEIR WAY TO THEIR OWN TIME MACHINE --

-- UNWITTINGLY MISSING PERHAPS ONE OF THE DARKEST MOMENTS IN THE HISTORY OF MANKIND.

NO TIME TO EXPLAIN! BEN, HANG ONTO ME!

JOHNNY... GRAB SUE! GET OUT... FAST!!

SO HELP ME, IF THIS IS ANOTHER GRANDSTAND PLAY...

AN EXPLOSION! FROM INSIDE THE SPHINX! WHAT HAPPENED, REED?

HECK, EVEN I CAN FIGURE IT OUT! IT WAS THE PHARAOH'S LAST BOOBY-TRAP! HE BLEW UP ALL HIS EQUIPMENT... EVERY LAST TRACE OF HIS EXISTENCE!

AS THEY RETURN TO THEIR PRESE THE FANTASTIC FOUR CANNOT SUS: WHO HAS TRULY DESTROYED TUT'S AND ITS CONTENTS.

THE DEVAST WROUGHT B EXPLOSION IMMENSE.

REPRESENTIN
THE ORIGIN,
COVERS TO

RISE OF
APOCALYP
#1-4

ADAM
POLLINA
—
MARK
MORALES
·1996·

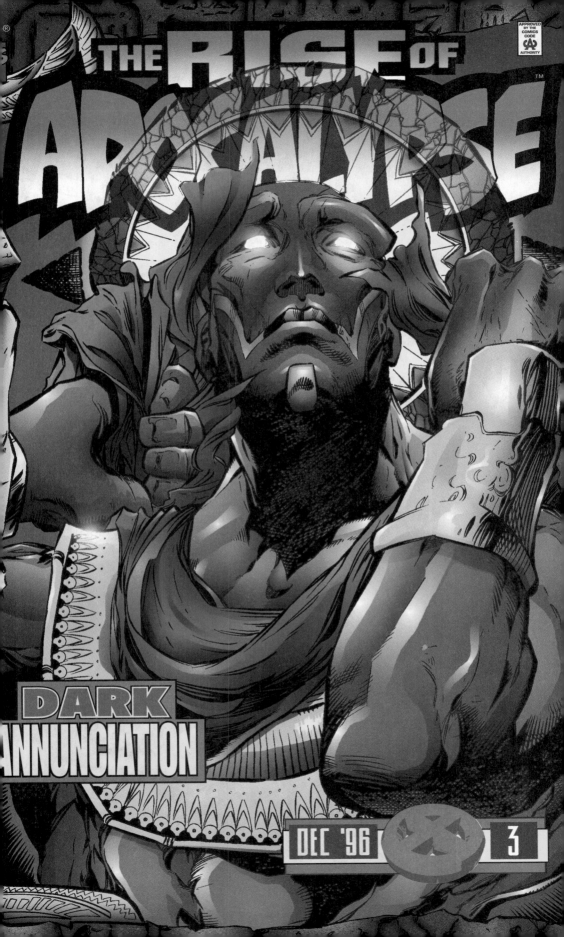

EXCERPTS FROM THE CHRONICLES
OF
OZYMANDIAS

"THUS DID I, SCRIBE OF THESE EVENTS— THE GREAT HISTORIC TABLEAU THAT IS THE STORY OF APOCALYPSE, COME TO BE IMPRISONED DEEP WITHIN THIS WONDROUS STRUCTURE. LAID LOW BY MY OWN PRIDE AND AMBITION— THAT OF A WARLORD— AND BLINDED TO HIS GREATNESS, SO SHALL I CONTINUE TO LABOR THROUGHOUT THE MILLENNIA AS IS MY WORTHY PUNISHMENT AND HUMBLE DESTINY.

TOO FOOLISH TO ACKNOWLEDGE HIS MAJESTY THEN, THESE INSCRIPTIONS ARE MY PERSONAL RECOMPENSE.

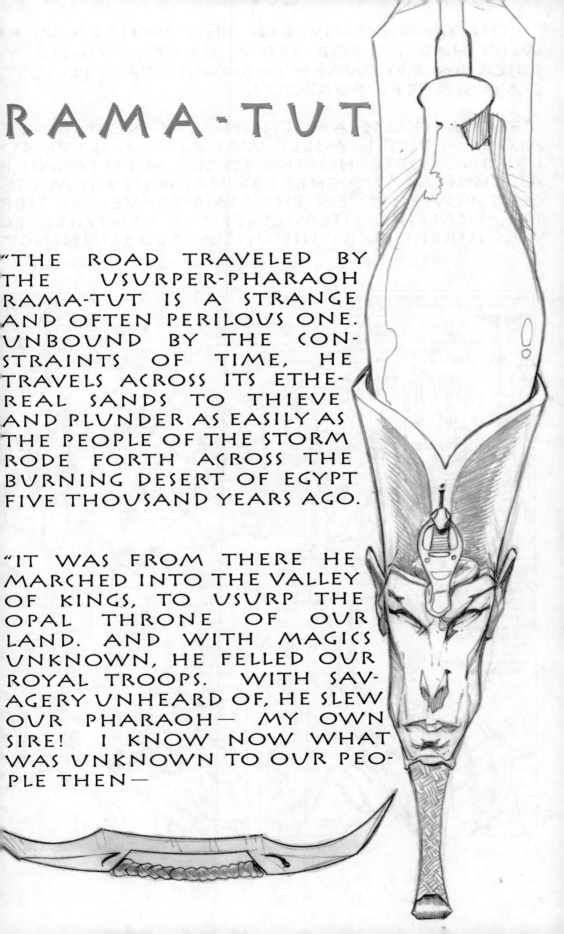

THE TRAVEL MOTIVES OF THE MYSTERIOUS...
WHO HAD PERFORMED A... IT... WALLED...
PLOT HE BATTLED THROUGH TIME TO SAVE
SWORTH OF PURPOSE.

...KILLS MAN... DON... THOUGHT
HIMSELF WAS BUT A SLAVE TO
... HOPING TO CLAIM EN PART...
... UP THE CRY, MANKIND BY WHOSE
POWER WHEN THE TIME-TRAVELER, HER
MOST ULTIMA... THE FANTASTIC...
MASTERING BY HIS VERY LIMIT TO OVERTHROW

RAMA-TUT

"THE ROAD TRAVELED BY THE USURPER-PHARAOH RAMA-TUT IS A STRANGE AND OFTEN PERILOUS ONE. UNBOUND BY THE CONSTRAINTS OF TIME, HE TRAVELS ACROSS ITS ETHEREAL SANDS TO THIEVE AND PLUNDER AS EASILY AS THE PEOPLE OF THE STORM RODE FORTH ACROSS THE BURNING DESERT OF EGYPT FIVE THOUSAND YEARS AGO.

"IT WAS FROM THERE HE MARCHED INTO THE VALLEY OF KINGS, TO USURP THE OPAL THRONE OF OUR LAND. AND WITH MAGICS UNKNOWN, HE FELLED OUR ROYAL TROOPS. WITH SAVAGERY UNHEARD OF, HE SLEW OUR PHARAOH— MY OWN SIRE! I KNOW NOW WHAT WAS UNKNOWN TO OUR PEOPLE THEN—

"—THE TRUE MOTIVES OF THIS MYSTERIOUS K[
WHO HAD PERFORMED A SIX–THOUSAND–Y
SOJOURN BACKWARD THROUGH TIME TO SUIT
OWN SINISTER PURPOSES.

"BUT RECKLESS AMBITION WAS NOT MY FO
ALONE— TUT HIMSELF WAS ALSO A SLAVE TO
DRIVING FORCE, HOPING TO CLAIM EN SABAH N
AS HIS HEIR AND THEREBY HARNESS HIS MAGN
CENT POWER. EVEN THE TIME-TRAVELING HER
TEAM CALLING THEMSELVES THE FANTASTIC FO
WAS SURPRISED BY HIS UNLIMITED CUNNING!"

MIND
EED AS
P AS
NCIENT
NDS
ED!
HIS

BUT *I* AM NOT A *PART* OF IT! AS YOU HAVE OBVIOUSLY GUESSED, NO ANCIENT PHARAOH FROM PRIMITIVE TIMES COULD HAVE THE POWER TO SUBDUE THE *FANTASTIC FOUR!*

THEN, THERE IS ONLY ONE POSSIBLE ANSWER, INCREDIBLE THOUGH IT MAY BE...

OF COURSE! *THIS* IS THE WEAPON THAT SAPPED YOUR POWERS, WHICH MADE YOU MY CAPTIVES!

THIS *ULTRA-DIODE RAY*, INVENTED IN THE YEAR 3000... ONE THOUSAND YEARS FURTHER IN THE FUTURE THAN YOUR *OWN* CENTURY!

THEN...YOU *TOO* ARE.. A *TIME TRAVELER!!*

9.

YES, I COME FROM THE YEAR 3000... THE GLORIOUS AGE OF ENLIGHTENMENT, THE CENTURY OF PEACE AND PROGRESS... THE ULTIMATE IN CIVILIZATION AND CULTURE! AND I *HATED* IT!

"FOR I WAS *THEN*, AS I AM *NOW*, A MAN OF *ACTION*, AN *ADVENTURER!* BUT THERE WERE NO ADVENTURES IN THE YEAR 3000 ...NO ENEMIES TO BATTLE, NO DRAGONS TO SLAY! ALL WAS PEACEFUL... HORRIBLY, UNBEARABLY PEACEFUL!!

WHY WAS I BORN INTO AN AGE WHEN THE ONLY EXCITEMENT A MAN CAN FIND IS IN WATCHING 3-D STEREOVISIONS FROM A THOUSAND YEARS AGO?!!

AS WHILE WATCHING SUCH ANCIENT FILMS, NTED BY OUR HISTORICAL SOCIETY, THAT I ED OF THE EXISTENCE OF THE *FANTASTIC* ! HOW I ENVIED YOUR DRAMATIC CAREERS!

"THEN, ONE DAY, WHILE VISITING THE RUINS OF AN AMAZING ANCESTOR OF MINE, I CAME UPON WHAT WAS LEFT OF HIS GREATEST INVENTION... A *TIME MACHINE!*

PART OF THE MACHINE STILL REMAINS....AND HERE ARE THE PLANS FOR ITS OPERATION!

IT WOULD BE SIMPLE FOR ME TO RECREATE IT AND USE IT FOR MY OWN PURPOSES!

"I DEVOTED YEARS TO THE BUILDING OF THAT TIME MACHINE, FROM MY ANCESTOR'S PLANS! BUT, KNOWING THE SUPERSTITIOUS BELIEFS OF PEOPLE IN BYGONE DAYS, I SHAPED IT IN THE FORM OF A STRANGE CREATURE, IN THE FORM OF AN *IDOL*!

"THEN AT LAST I WAS READY! READY TO TRAVE[L] LONG DEAD AGES... READY TO BECOME A T[IME] *LOOTER*, WITH MY HEADQUARTERS IN ANCIE[NT] EGYPT, WHERE, WITH MY VAST SCIENTIFIC KNO[W]LEDGE, I COULD BECOME AN ABSOLUTE RULER [OF] MANKIND!!

"AND SO I TRAVELED BACK INTO THE DIM PAST, BACK TO THE LAND OF ANCIENT EGYPT, IN MY MARVELOUS TIM[E] MACHINE, THAT WAS SHAPED LIKE AN AWESOME IDOL!

OH, WONDER OF WONDERS! WHAT *MIRACLE* IS UPON US??

"BUT, DUE TO A CARELESS MISCALCULATION ON MY PART, THE MACHINE WAS *DAMAGED* IN LANDING, SO THAT I HAVE BEEN UNABLE TO LEAVE THIS PRIMITIVE CENTURY! ALSO, I SUFFERED A TERRIBLE INJURY AS I CRASHED!

MY *EYES*!! I CAN'T *SEE*!!

"BUT, FIRING BLINDLY AT THE DAZED NATIVES, I MAD[E] THEM MY SLAVES! THEY OBTAINED A RARE HERB[?] FOR ME THAT AFFECTED BY THE RADIATION FROM MY DAMAGED MACHINE, HAD THE POWER TO REST[ORE] MY EYESIGHT! I HAVE RULED HERE EVER SINCE!"

AND NOW, MY BRIDE-TO-BE, SIP YOUR NECTAR AND TOAST OUR LOVE, FOR SOON YOU SHALL BE QUEEN OF ALL THE NILE!

GUESS AGAIN, LOVER BOY!

I DID IT! NOW I'VE GOT THAT GUN OF YOURS, AND THINGS ARE GONNA START POPPIN' AROUND HERE!

ANOTHER TWENTIETH CENTURY INTRUDER! BUT WHO? HOW? UGH!!

ONCE AWAY FROM THE BURNING RAYS OF THE IVE DESERT SUN, BEN GRIMM BEGINS TO RT TO HIS OTHER FORM... AND, AS HE SLOWLY G INTO THE THING, HE FEELS HIMSELF AGAIN G UNDER THE WILL-SAPPING INFLUENCE OF HARAOH'S RAY GUN! AND SO...

MUST FREE SUE BEFORE I GO UNDER... CAN'T LET MY ESCAPE HAVE BEEN IN VAIN! MUSTN'T MISS... JUST ONE BLAST... JUST ONE...

THE RAYS STRUCK HER A SECOND TIME! SHE'S NORMAL AGAIN! MUST GET THE GUN FROM HER!

YOU SAVED ME, BEN! NOW I HAVE THE GUN! IT'S UP TO ME... AND I WON'T LET YOU DOWN! I WON'T FAIL THE FANTASTIC FOUR!

ME THAT RAY GUN, ! IT WON'T HELP 'LL SEIZE IT E YOU CAN LEARN TO OPERATE IT!

I'VE GOT TO STALL FOR TIME! EVEN A FEW SECONDS!

YOU ARE ELUSIVE, MY QUEEN-TO-BE! BUT TURNING INVISIBLE WILL DO NO GOOD! I CAN STILL SEE YOUR GARMENTS!

I FORGOT! I'M NOT WEARING MY UNSTABLE-MOLECULE COSTUME! ONLY ONE CHANCE LEFT.. I'LL FIRE AT THE TORCH!

"HE WOULD SURELY HAVE SPENT AN ETERNITY IN THE UNDERWORLD
MEETING THE WRATH OF EN SABAH NUR. HE KNOWS NOT THE TERRIBLE
HE ESCAPED THAT DAY."

"NEITHER REED RICHARDS, THE LEADER OF THE BRAVE QUARTET, NO
WOULD EVER SUSPECT THAT I, OZYMANDIAS, WAS LEFT HERE TO RE
THOSE EXPLOITS."

"AND WHAT OF MY OWN SISTER NEPHRI—

"—SHE WHO HAD GONE ON TO BECOME EGYPT'S QUEEN AFTER SPURNING MY LORD? HER CORPSE HAS LONG SINCE WASTED AWAY AND SHE NOW WALKS IN THE AFTERLIFE.

"PERHAPS HAD SHE EMBRACED EN SABAH NUR, SHE WOULD HAVE TAUGHT HIM HUMANITY'S WORTH AND THE VALUE OF LOVE. INSTEAD, HER PRE-JUDICE HASTENED HIM ON HIS RISE...

"...AND SEALED MANKIND'S FATE.

"AND HE WHO WAS ONCE A HUNTED OUT-CAST— ONCE A MERE DESERT NOMAD NAMED EN SABAH NUR— SHALL STRIDE FORTH TO CRUSH ALL MEN BENEATH HIS HEEL AS IS HIS DESTINY. HE PAVES THE WAY FOR ALL MUTANTKIND AND HIS KIND OF MUTANT ALONE. ONLY THE FIT SHALL SURVIVE HIS ARRIVAL.

"SO IT WAS THAT MY LORD BIDED HIS TIME THROUGHOUT THE AGES TO FOLLOW, THE FIRST OF HIS KIND, AWAITING THE SLOW EMERGENCE OF HIS GENETIC BRETHREN INTO THE WORLD...

"BUT THIS ADVENT DID NOT FULLY COME TO PASS UNTIL THE TWENTIETH CENTURY. APOCALYPSE HAD WATCHED MAN GROW STRONG OVER THE PASSING YEARS, BECOMING CAPABLE EVEN OF DESTROYING HIS OWN PLANET. APOCALYPSE WAS AWARE THAT MAN WAS BECOMING MORE AND MORE CUNNING CENTURY AFTER CENTURY. THE MUTANT STRAIN OF HUMANITY COULD NOT HAVE PICKED A MORE OPPORTUNE TIME TO MANIFEST ITSELF, AND NOW WAS THE MOMENT FOR MY LORD TO RISE AGAIN AT LONG LAST!

"AND LET NO ONE, MAN OR MUTANT, DEFY HIS WILL— FOR FROM IT, THERE IS NO ESCAPE!"

WWW-- ON, YS!

WHAT DO YOU THINK, JEANIE? SHOULD I FLY UP AND GET 'IM?

NO. I THINK THERE'S A FASTER WAY TO BRING BOBBY DOWN!

SHRAKT!

HANG ON, BOBBY! I'LL GET YOU DOWN-- REAL FAST!

HELLLLPP!

OH, DON'T BE SUCH A BABY! I'VE GOT YOU! BUT SINCE YOU INSIST ON BEING WET BE-HIND THE EARS PERHAPS--

-- YOU COULD USE A SPIN-DRY!

YEEOOWWWW!

BELIEVE HE'S D ENOUGH, JEAN!

WELL, IF THAT'S SO --HOW ABOUT AN APOLOGY TO MR. McCOY, BOBBY?

ORRY, L' BUDDY! Y PLEASE'? MAKE ME ROUGH AIN!

GY TED, OSTY NION!

EVERYTHING SEEMS SO RIGHT WITH US-- LIKE OLD TIMES. BUT IT ISN'T--THINGS HAVE CHANGED AND I KEEP WONDERING-- ARE WE LIVING A LIE?

SOME THREE THOUSAND MILES WESTWARD SITS THE TOMAHAWK MOTOR LODGE! WITHIN ONE OF THE SEEDY APARTMENTS, THE ODOR OF MILDEWED CARPETING MINGLES WITH--

--THE SMELL OF FEAR AS A TREMBLING HAND DESPERATELY ATTEMPTS TO COM-PLETE A CALL!

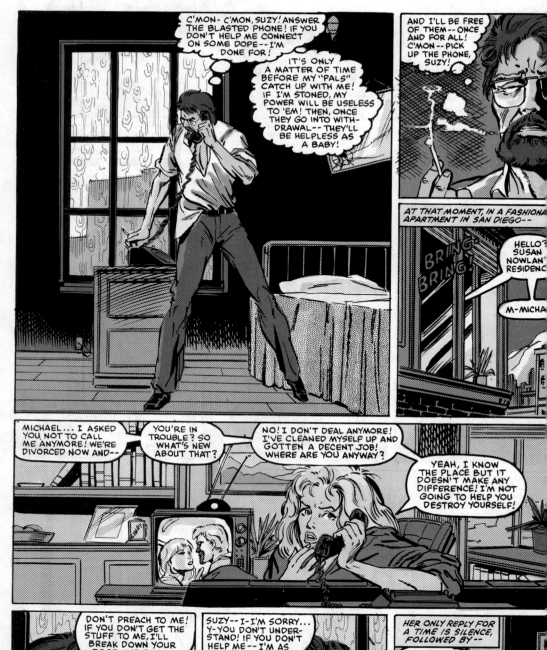

TROUBLED BY MUTANTS! WELL-- YOU NO LONGER HAVE CAUSE TO FEAR! FOR NOW THERE'S --

...AM ...NG TO ...E'S ...GH ...NCE!

...'S ...?

-- X-FACTOR! PROFESSIONAL INVESTIGATORS, WHO WITH TODAY'S ADVANCED TECHNOLOGY, CAN PROTECT YOU AND YOUR FAMILY FROM THIS UNSEEN MENACE! CALL THIS TOLL-FREE NUMBER NOW AND LET THE MUTANT PROFESSIONALS HANDLE IT! YOU DON'T HAVE TO LIVE IN FEAR ANYMORE!

AFTER A FEW MOMENTS OF ANGUISHED DECISION MAKING--

HELLO-- X-FACTOR? I HAVE A PROBLEM!

...WHILE, IN A CHIC NEW-WAVE BOUTIQUE IN THE ...ON OF NEW YORK CITY KNOWN AS SOHO--

I DON'T THINK HE'S GONNA COME OUT OF THERE, VERA!

WE'LL SEE ABOUT THAT, BOBBY DRAKE!

HANKY-POO-- PLEASE COME OUT! I WANT TO SEE WHAT YOU LOOK LIKE IN YOUR NEW CLOTHES!

I LOOK RIDICULOUS! I'M A RESPECTED BIO-PHYSICIST! WHAT IF ONE OF MY COLLEAGUES SAW ME LIKE THIS?

...BE SILLY, HANK! NO SELF-...ECTING SCIENTIST WOULD ...UGHT DEAD IN SOHO!

THAT TEARS IT!!!

...JUST ...NG, ...IE! IF ...OVE ME ...ASE ...OUT!

NOW, THAT'S NOT FAIR, VERA!

EXCUSE ME-- IS THERE A PROBLEM? YOUR FRIEND HAS BEEN IN THERE FOR AN AWFULLY LONG TIME!

EVERYTHING IS ALL RIGHT, MISS! MY BUDDY IS JUST NOT USED TO BEING A "FASHION RISK!"

YUPPIES-- YUCH!

THAT'S A GOOD BOY, HANK! I'LL BET YOU LOOK SO SEXY!

⋛SIGH⋚ THE THINGS I DO FOR LOVE...!

MR. SUMMERS--IF THERE IS ...HING ARTHUR OR I CAN DO TO HELP, WE'LL BE--

NO, IT'S NOTHING BOTH OF YOU HAVE BEEN PERFORMING EXCELLENTLY OF LATE. MY MIND IS ON OTHER MATTERS TODAY. WHY DON'T YOU --EH?

BEEP! BEEP! BEEP!

THAT WILL BE ALL FOR TODAY, BOYS! I HAVE TO REPORT FOR A BRIEFING. WE'LL-- PICK UP WHERE WE LEFT OFF TOMORROW!

AH... SURE THING, MR. SUMMERS! SEE YOU TOMORROW!

AFTER CYCLOPS DEPARTS--

I DON'T GET IT, ARTIE! THAT GUY SEEMS TO HAVE EVERYTHING GOING FOR HIM! WHY IS HE ALWAYS SUCH A 'GLOOMY GUS'?

THE MUTE LAD PONDERS WHETHER TO SHOW RUSTY WHAT HE KNOWS. THEN, THE MUTANT'S EYES BEGIN TO GLOW, AND --

...IMAGES APPEAR! ...NSFIXED RUSTY ...'S AS VISIONS OF ...GREY, SCOTT'S ... LOVE AND MADELYNE ... HIS ESTRANGED ... PARADE BEFORE ...ARTHUR CEASES TO ...OJECT, THEN--

I--I'M NOT SURE WHAT THAT ALL MEANS, ARTIE! I RECOGNIZED MISS GREY, BUT THAT OTHER WOMAN--WHO WAS SHE? SHOULD WE TALK TO JEAN?

BUT ARTIE, WHO KNOWS ALL SCOTT'S SORROWS AND HEARTACHE, SHAKES HIS HEAD FIRMLY: NO!

MEANWHILE, IN ANOTHER SECTION OF THE X-FACTOR COMPLEX--

HI, WARREN! HOLDING DOWN THE FORT?

I WAS WORRIED ABOUT YOU, JEAN! YOU'VE BEEN GONE QUITE SOME TIME! WHAT'S UP?

WARREN, I'M NOT A PIECE OF CHINA! I CAN TAKE CARE OF MYSELF, YOU KNOW!

OOOPS! SORRY... 'COLLEGE TEXT BOOKS? ADVANCED PSYCHOLOGY? WHAT'S THIS?

WELL, I DECIDED IT WAS TIME TO GET ON WITH MY LIFE, SO --

...NROLLED IN ...T CLASSES ...OLUMBIA! I ...RED THAT A ...EE IN PSY- ...OGY COULD ... IN HANDY ...R LINE ...ORK!

IT ALSO MIGHT HELP ME UNDERSTAND THE MOTIVATIONS OF CERTAIN INDIVIDUALS AROUND HERE.

IF YOU'RE REFERRING TO A CERTAIN SCOTT SUMMERS--I'M AFRAID IT'S GOING TO TAKE MORE THAN A B.A. IN PSYCHOLOGY!

THEN, WHY DON'T YOU TELL ME WHAT IT WILL TAKE TO GET HIM TO OPEN UP TO ME AGAIN? I'M BEGINNING TO FEEL LIKE A SOCIAL OUTCAST AROUND HE--

EH?

ALL X-FACTOR MEMBERS-- REPORT FOR BRIEFING IMMEDIATELY!

IT'LL HAVE TO WAIT, JEAN! LET'S MOVE!

GATHERING IN THE CONFERENCE ROOM, X-FACTOR IS BRIEFED ON THEIR ASSIGNMENT BY X-FACTOR'S ADMINISTRATOR, CAMERON HODGE.

ALTHOUGH SUZY NOWLAN'S INFORMATION WAS SKETCHY, I BELIEVE THIS CASE WARRANTS INVESTIGATION!

CAMERON--IF THIS MICHAEL NOWLAN IS INVOLVED IN DRUG ABUSE, HOW DO WE KNOW IF THIS ISN'T MERELY A PSYCHOTIC EPISODE--A DELUSION BROUGHT ON BY NARCOTICS USE?

I AGREE! WE DON'T EVEN KNOW WHAT POWER THIS NOWLAN ALLEGEDLY POSSESSES?

THAT'S TRUE, BUT THERE'S MORE TO IT, PEOPLE!

MS. NOWLAN [IN]FORMED ME T[HAT] MICHAEL HAS BE[EN] IN THE COMPANY [OF] OTHER MUTANT[S] FOR SOME TIM[E] NOW! FROM HE[R] DESCRIPTIONS, [SOME] OF THEM SOU[ND] DISTURBINGLY

--FRENZY AND OUR OLD FRIEND-- TOWER!

GREAT SCOTT! DO YOU THINK THIS MIGHT HAVE A CONNECTION WITH THE ATTEMPT TO ABDUCT RUSTY LAST WEEK?*

* SEE ISSUE #4. --BOB.

HARD TO SAY, HANK! BUT THEIR INVOLVEMENT DOES LEND CREDENCE TO THE CASE, WOULDN'T YOU SAY?

IF NOWLAN IS A TRUE HOMO-SUPERIOR, WE CAN'T ALLOW HIM TO FALL INTO THE HANDS OF THOSE EVIL MUTANTS!

AGREED! I MOVE WE LEAVE IM[MEDI]ATELY FOR SAN DIEGO! TIME M[AY] NOT BE ON OUR SIDE, IN THIS [CASE]

LET'S GOING, T[EAM]

AT THAT MOMENT IN SAN DIEGO, SUZY NOWLAN HAS MADE A SIMILAR DECISION--

I'VE GOT TO GET OUT OF HERE!

I CAN'T SIT AROUND HERE WAITING FOR MICHAEL TO TURN MY LIFE UPSIDE-DOWN AGAIN!

I'LL JUST SKIP T[OWN] AND START OVE[R] WITHOUT TELLI[NG] ANYONE THAT

--GOING SOMEWHERE, SUZY?!

OHHHH!

I THINK NOT, MY DEAR! NOT UNTIL YOU TALK!

SWAK!

OOOOFFF!!

NO...NOT YOU! GET OUT OF MY LIFE, FREAKS!!

KS? OH, LIKE-- THAT'S A DIE THING TO FOR SURE!

SHUT UP, STINGER!

THE JUNKIE, SUZY! WHERE IS HE?

YOU'D BETTER TELL US, DEAR! I'M AFRAID WE'RE QUITE DESPERATE!

G-GOT TO MAKE A BREAK FOR IT!

THE PANIC-STRICKEN WOMAN MAKES A MAD SCRAMBLE TO THE DOOR, ONLY TO FIND--

OH...NO!

HIYA, SUZY-Q! I THINK YOU'D BETTER TELL FRENZY WHAT SHE WANTS TA KNOW!

AN FORGET ABOUT WINDOWS, GIRL! YOU'D GET PAST TIME- OW'S PHASE-FORMS!

HELP! OMEBODY...!

ENOUGH! YOU WILL TELL ME WHERE NOWLAN IS OR--

--I'LL CRUSH THE LIFE FROM YOUR WEAK HUMAN BODY!

MEANWHILE, AT SAN DIEGO AIRPORT, A LIMO IS LOWERED FROM THE BELLY OF X-FACTOR'S MOBILE HEADQUARTERS.

A SHORT TIME LATER, OUTSIDE THE TOMAHAWK MOTOR LODGE--

IT'S NOT LIKELY THAT NOWLAN WOULD CHANCE GOING OUT! NOT IF HE'S BEING HOUNDED!

I DON'T SEE ANY ALTERNATIVE!

THAT'S ODD! THIS I THE PLACE MRS. NOW TOLD CAMERON ABOU BUT THERE'S NO ANSWER!

SHALL WE FORCE THE DOOR

ARE YOU SURE, SCOTT? IT DOESN'T SEEM RIGHT

IF WE INTERRUPT A HONEYMOONING COUPLE, WE'LL BUY THEM SOME CHAMPAGNE LATER! OPEN IT UP, JEAN!

SCOTT ...I--

DO IT!

RELUCTANTLY, MARVEL GIRL USES HER TELE-KINETIC POWERS TO UNLOCK THE DOOR MECHANISM.

CLICK!

IT'S OPEN-- I'LL THAN NOT TO Y ME AGA

JEAN, I'M...LET'S SEE WHO'S HOME!

12

THE DOOR SWINGS OPEN TO REVEAL--

12

OH, NO!

NOWLAN!

SCOTT-- IS HE...?

DEAD? NO, BUT IT L LIKE HE FOUND HIM ANOTHER CONNECTI

S WH W N

HANK-- SEE WHAT YOU CAN DO TO BRING HIM OUT OF IT! WE NEED HIM CON- SCIOUS TO ANSWER SOME QUESTIONS!

A FEW IMPATIENT... THE BEAST IS ...SSFUL IN HIS ATTEMPT ...IVE NOWLAN.

MR. NOWLAN--TAKE ...T EASY. WE'D LIKE ...O ASK YOU A FEW QUESTIONS!

WAIT A MINUTE! WHO ARE YOU? HOW'D YOU GET IN?

WE'RE X-FACTOR! WE'RE HERE TO HELP YOU, MICHAEL!

X-FACTOR! I-I'VE HEARD OF YOU GUYS! Y-YOU'RE MUTANT EXTERMINATORS OR SOMETHING LIKE THAT!

NO! IT'S NOT LIKE THAT AT ALL! HEAR US OUT!

NO! STAY AWAY FROM ME! I WON'T LET YOU TAKE ME!

EVERYONE-- STAND BACK! SOMETHING'S HAPPENING TO HIM!

...NLY, TENDRILS OF ENERGY LEAP FROM NOWLAN, CAUSING ...OF THE MUTANTS' POWERS TO RUN AMOK!

JEAN!!

SCOTT!

T-TELEKINESIS --OUT--OF CONTROL!

O-OPTIC... BLASTS...TOO STRONG TO H-HOLD!

ARRGGH! CAN'T...SHUT... POWERS...OFF...

...ERGY DISSIPATES, ...G IN ITS WAKE --

...ARE NOT ...EYES...GOT ...ND VISOR ...MUCH POWER!

EASY, SCOTT! I'VE GOT YOUR GLASSES!

POWERS...RETURNING TO NORMAL...!

ICEMAN-- POWER DOWN! YOU'RE PLUNGING THE ROOM TO SUB-ZERO!

MUTANTS! YOU GUYS ARE MUTANTS TOO! I DON'T GET IT! WHAT'S THE SCAM? YOU OUT TO DESTROY YOUR OWN KIND?

TAKE IT EASY, BUDDY! GIVE US A CHANCE TO EXPLAIN EVERYTHING! MIGHT AS WELL CHANGE NOW THAT OUR CLOTHES ARE IN TATTERS. JUST HEAR US OUT!

WITH AN UNEASY NOD OF APPROVAL FROM MICHAEL, SCOTT SUMMERS BEGINS TO RELATE THE PURPOSE OF X-FACTOR AND THE EVENTS THAT HAVE BROUGHT THEM TO THIS CONFRONTATION.

AS CYCLOPS CONCLUDES--

I GOTTA HAND IT TO YA-- IT'S A SET-UP! BUT IT DOESN'T DO ME A GOOD! NO ONE CAN HELP ME!

I DON'T UNDERSTAND Y MICHAEL! WHY DO YOU ON DESTROYING YOURS WITH DRUGS? DON'T Y KNOW WHAT YOU'RE DOING TO YOURSELF

ALL TOO WELL, RED! BUT IT'S THE ONLY THING THAT MAKES ME USELESS TO MUTANTS-- IT RETARDS THE POWER!

"I GOT HOOKED LONG BEFORE I WAS SENT HOME FROM 'NAM! THE ARMY PUT ME IN A MILITARY DE-TOX CENTER TO DRY OUT! THEY COULDN'T BE RELEASING *THEIR* JUNKIES ON AN UNSUSPECTING CIVILIAN POPULACE, NOW COULD THEY?

"SUZY AND I WERE STILL TO- GETHER THEN-- CLEANIN' UP OUR ACT!

"WHAT I DIDN'T KNOW IS THAT MY POWER HAD MANIFESTED ITSELF WHILE I WAS DOPED UP! IT STAYED DORMANT THROUGH MY LATE TEENS BECAUSE OF THE DRUGS!

"A SHORT TIME AF ENTERIN' DE-TOX, I FELLOW PATIENT I WARD!

"ALL I DID WA HIS HAND

--"WHAMMO! HE WAS A MUTANT AND, BABY-- DID HIS POWER GO WILD!"

...Y, AFTER THAT
...NT, THE WORD
...STREETS ABOUT
...ITY TO AUGMENT
...T ENERGIES! THINGS
...FROM BAD TO WORSE
...ANTS STARTED
...G ME OUT-- THEY
...OKED ON THE
...LIKE A DRUG!
...E ONLY THING
...ADE ME
...S TO
...VAS--

--PUTTING THAT JUNK BACK IN MY VEINS! IT RETARDS THE ENERGY TRANSFER! BUT IT'S LOST ME MY WIFE-- MY HEALTH-- MY FREAKIN' SANITY! I DON'T WANT THIS!

MIKE-- WE CAN HELP YOU, IF YOU'LL ONLY--

TRUST YOU, RIGHT? WELL --FORGET IT, LADY! EVERYTIME I TRUSTED A "FELLOW MUTANT," THEY WIND UP A POWER JUNKIE AND I GET THE SHORT END OF THE STICK! NO THANKS!

GREAT! THIS GUY WOULD RATHER POISON HIMSELF TO DEATH THAN LET US HELP HIM! WHAT ARE WE GOING TO DO? WE CAN'T LET HIM FALL INTO THE WRONG HANDS!

I HATE TO SAY IT BUT-- PERHAPS WE SHOULD LET HIM STAY HIGH! IF ONLY TO ELIMINATE THE POSSIBILITY OF SOMEONE GAINING CONTR--

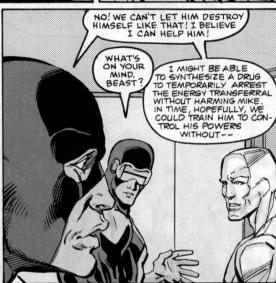

NO! WE CAN'T LET HIM DESTROY HIMSELF LIKE THAT! I BELIEVE I CAN HELP HIM!

WHAT'S ON YOUR MIND, BEAST?

I MIGHT BE ABLE TO SYNTHESIZE A DRUG TO TEMPORARILY ARREST THE ENERGY TRANSFERRAL WITHOUT HARMING MIKE. IN TIME, HOPEFULLY, WE COULD TRAIN HIM TO CONTROL HIS POWERS WITHOUT--

I'M NOT LETTIN' ...ODY USE ME FOR ...NEA PIG AGAIN!

I'M GETTIN' THE BLAZE OUTTA HERE! YOU GUYS CAN GO TO THE DEVIL!

MIKE-- DON'T! HEAR US OUT!

NO WAY, APE-MAN!

MIKE! STOP IT! LISTEN TO ME!

WHERE ARE YOU GOING TO GO? HOW ARE YOU GOING TO HIDE FROM YOURSELF? IF YOU DON'T LET ME HELP--YOU'LL BE DEAD IN A MATTER OF MONTHS!

OR WORSE YET-- IF YOU FALL INTO THE WRONG HANDS, YOU'LL SPEND THE REST OF YOUR LIFE AS A SLAVE TO OTHERS' UN-CONTROLLABLE HUNGERS! IS THAT WHAT YOU WANT? IS IT?

NO-- NO! PLEASE-- HELP ME!

I -- WE WILL. I PROMISE! EVERYTHING IS GOING TO BE--

KERCHOO

WELL, LOOKIE HERE! ALL MY OLD PLAYMATES-- ALL IN ONE PLACE! I THINK THIS IS GONNA BE FUN!

OH, NO! NOT NOW!

M-MIKE-- I'M SORRY! T-THEY MADE ME--

LET HER GO, TOWER! SHE'S NOTHIN' TO YOU JERKS!

WANNA BET, LOUD MOUTH? SHE'S INSURANCE! YOU GIVE US THE 'JUICE' OR FRENZY'LL PLAY 'THE EXORCIST' WITH LIL' SUZY'S HEAD!

NO!

DON'T DO IT NOW WE'LL SAVE THE G DON'T HELP THEM THEY'RE BLUFFIN

IZZAT WHAT YOU THINK, BUG-EYES?

TIMESHADOW'S THE NAME, WOMAN! EVEN WITH YOUR FORMIDABLE ABILITIES, YOU CAN'T POSSIBLY DISTINGUISH MY PHASE-FORMS FROM THE REAL ME! I'M ALWAYS A MILI-SECOND AHEAD OF YOU!

I WON'T HAVE TO, TIMESHADOW! I'LL SIMPLY--

--TAKE ON ALL SIX OF YOU AT ONCE!

CHOOM!

CHOOM!

CHOOM!

CHOOM!

CHOOM!

CHOOM!

NOT QUITE, MY DEAR! I MERELY--

--PHASED OUT OF TIME-SYNC FOR A SPLIT SECOND!

PLEASANT DREAMS, BEAUTIFUL!

WHAP!

MARVEL GIRL!!

YOU TREACHEROUS SCUM! I'LL BLAST YOU OUT OF EXISTENCE!

SHRRAAK!

C'MON, STINGER-- LET'S FINISH THIS CREEP OFF!

I DON'T CARE HOW MUCH YOUR POWERS ARE AUGMENTED BY THAT JUNKIE! YOU'LL FIND I'M--

--MORE THAN YOU CAN HANDLE!!

SHRRAAKK!!

WHAM!

GUESS AGAIN, CYCLOPS! YOU'RE FINISHED!

THE ROOM IS SILENT FOR A MOMENT. THEN--

OKAY, NOWLAN -- WHAT'S IT GONNA BE? DO WE KILL THEM AND THE GIRL RIGHT HERE OR--

NO...NO, YOU WIN! I'M YOURS! JUST NO MORE KILLIN'!

"THEY WON'T GIVE YOU ANY MORE TROUBLE."

THEY'RE FINISHED!

OURS LATER,
CHATEAU
T ALL BEGAN--

MASTER-- WE HAVE BROUGHT HIM BACK, AS YOU INSTRU--

NCE, ZY! YOU E THE US!

STEP CLOSER, BOY.

YOU HAVE CAUSED ME CONSIDERABLE GRIEF, ADDICT! I HAVE HAD TO DELAY MY PLANS, AT NOT SOME SMALL INCONVENIENCE TO MYSELF! SO MARK MY WORDS WELL, BOY!

YOU WILL RETURN TO MY LABORATORY, WHERE I SHALL COMPLETE MY EXPERIMENTS ON YOU! IF YOU FAIL TO COOPERATE--

-- THE GIRL DIES.

IF YOU CHOOSE TO ESCAPE AGAIN--

--THE GIRL DIES.

M-MASTER ...I...

ENOUGH! THE TIME IS NEARLY AT HAND AND I WILL BROOK NO INTERFERENCE! YOU SHALL SOON PROVIDE ALL MUTANT-KIND WITH A SOURCE OF UNLIMITED MIGHT-- A RACE OF SUPER-MUTANTS! AND I SHALL LEAD THEM TO WAR AGAINST THE PUNY INFECTION CALLED --MAN!

SO SWEARS APOCALYPSE!

'T E: THE MENACE OF APOCALYPSE!!

TOMAHAWK MOTOR LODGE

COLOR TV AIR COND. X-RATED MOVIES **YES**

HEY! SERGEANT! SERGEANT GORELLI!

YEAH, SIMSKY, WHAT'S YOUR PROBLEM?

THAT PILE OF *RUBBLE'S* MY PROBLEM!

THAT *LIMO* PULLS UP AN' THEM GUYS IN *UNIFORMS* STALK INTO MY MOTEL, AN' I KNOW I GOT TROUBLE!

HOW COME SAN DIEGO'S FINEST LETS *MUTIES* SMASH UP HONEST MEN'S PROPERTY?

HONEST JOE SIMSKY, HUH? THAT'S A NEW ONE! LAST TIME SOMEBODY TRASHED YOUR ROACH MOTEL, YOU DIDN'T WANT COPS ANYWHERE *NEAR!*

HOW COME YOU CALLED US IN ON *THIS* ONE?

SHOW 'IM THAT AD FROM THE PAPER, RUBY!

X-FACTOR

MUTANT INVESTIGATIONS A[ND] RESOLUTIONS! NO NEED TO BE FEARFUL A[NY] LONGER! OUR SKILLED TEA[M] OF *EXPERTS* WILL AID YOU [IN] FINDING THE ANSWERS TO [...] OF THE MOST URGENT PRO[B]LEMS OF OUR TIME! CALL OUR TOLL-FREE NUM[BER] OPERATORS STANDING BY!

THESE'RE THE GUYS FROM THE LIMO, SERGEANT!

THEY WENT INSIDE AND SOME *MUTIES* CRASHED IN AFTER 'EM!

THERE WAS THIS *EXPLOSION*, SEE, AN' SOUNDS OF A WHOP-PIN' *FIGHT!* AN' THEN THE MUTIES CRASHED *OUT!*

PROBABLY *KILLED* THOSE X-FACTOR GUYS!

BLASTED VIGILANTE *BOUNTY HUNTERS!*

SOMEBODY'S GOTTA STOP THEM *MUTIES!* AN' SOME OF 'EM MIGHT STILL BE *IN* THERE!

I PAY TAXES AN' I'M ENTITL[ED] TO *PROTECTIO[N]* LIKE EVERYBO[DY] ELSE!

SO GO ON, GORELLI! GE[T] IN THERE AN[D] *PROTECT* ME!

...AND I'M NOT A *TELE-PATH* ANYMORE! I'VE *TRIED* TO TELL MYSELF THAT I HAVE *OTHER* POWERS-- THAT IT DOESN'T MATTER--

-- BUT IT *DOES!*

COULD READ PEOPLE'S ELINGS... THEIR *THOUGHTS*... AND NOW IT'S LIKE I'M A *JAR* WITH THE LID CREWED ON TIGHT!

YOU'VE CHANGED! YOU ACT LIKE YOU *HATE* ME-- YOU'RE *KEEPING* THINGS FROM ME... BUT I DON'T KNOW *WHAT...*

...AND I DON'T KNOW *WHY!*

JEAN! JEANIE! STOP! LISTEN!

'S *NOT* YOU! 'S *SCOTT!*

I'VE TRIED TO BE UNDERSTAND-ING, BUT WITH ALL SHE'S *BEEN* THROUGH, WITH ALL SHE *WAS* TO YOU, DOESN'T SHE DESERVE TO KNOW THE *TRUTH?*

THE *TRUTH*... AS IF *YOU* WOULD UNDER-STAND!

BUT THEN, IT WAS *YOUR* IDEA TO FORM *X-FACTOR,* WASN'T IT? TO PRETEND TO BE *MUTANT HUNTERS,* TO USE THOSE STUPID *ADS* TO LOCATE MUTANTS...

...THEN TEACH THEM TO CONTROL THEIR POWERS SO THEY'LL NO LONGER *MENACE* A SOCIETY THAT HATES AND *FEARS* THEM...

...OT TO ...TION ...MESS MELT-...ICE ...MAKE?

NO PROBLEM, M'MAN!

THAT OUGHTA TAKE CARE OF IT!

OF ALL THE SHOW OFF, PLAYBOY STUNTS!

LIGHTEN UP, SCOTT! IT'S NOT LIKE THE PLACE IS IN GREAT SHAPE TO BEGIN WITH!

I REALLY THINK THE LANDLORD WOULD RATHER HAVE THE CASH!

IF MY FINANCIAL ...ATION WORRIES ...REIMBURSE ME...

...RIGHT, JEANIE?

HA-HA! RIGHT!

THE POLICEMAN'S INCHING TOWARD THE DOOR!

OR WHAT REMAINS OF IT!

CONSIDERING HOW SCARED OF US THEY ALL ARE, THAT COP IS ONE BRAVE DUDE!

C-CONNECTION? NO CONNECTION, FRENZY! YOU GOTTA BELIEVE ME! YOU GOT ME NOW! PLEASE...PLEASE LET SUZIE GO!

SHE TRIED TO HELP ME KICK THE HABIT... STRAIGHTEN OUT MY LIFE! SHE BELIEVED IN ME! I'M NOT WORTH WHAT IT'S DONE TO HER! I'M NOT...

I DON'T DISPUTE THAT, ADDICT!

YOUR LOVER HAS ESCAPED PERMANENT INJURY... SO FAR! BUT SHE IS IN DANGER, MICHAEL, UNLESS YOU COOPERATE!

BUT-- I DON'T KNOW ANYTHING...THEY JUST WANTED TO HELP ME... THEY...PLEASE...I NEED A FIX, GOTTA HAVE--

WHAKT!

UGH!

TWO LOSER, E MAN-- ANT E!

YOU OUGHTA HAVE NO PROBLEM BE-TRAYIN' YOUR NEW PALS! YOU DID ONCE ALREADY, DIDN'T YOU?

NOW WHO ARE THEY? WHO ARE THEY?!?

ALL RIGHT, TOWER... I-I'LL TELL!

RE NTS, S!

THEY'VE BANDED TO-GETHER TO FIGHT MUTANT HUNTERS LIKE X-FACTOR... THEY DROVE THEM OFF...

THAT'S ALL! NOW, PLEASE... PLEASE...

LIKE... THERE'S MORE TO IT, FER SURE, AN' YOU GOTTA TELL US!

IT'S A COINCIDENCE, THAT THEY'VE SHOWED UP WHEN WE TRIED TO NAB YOU?

YES... A...A CO-INCIDENCE! PLEASE, TIMESHADOW! THE DRUGS... I...I NEED THEM! I... I...HURT...!

BUT THAT WILL BLOCK HIS POWER! WHY SHOULD I BE *WEAKENED* WHILE THIS ADDICT--?

BECAUSE *I* HAVE *COMMANDED* IT, FRENZY!

KNEEL BEFORE YOUR MASTER-- AND KNOW THAT IF HE CHOSE IT, *APOCALYPSE* COULD DESTROY YOU!

WHAK!

CONTROL ... DY-- RE- ... GE AND ... RUCTURE ... OLECULES ... UITS ME!

... GTH-- ... INVULNER- ... Y, ARE ... NG COM- ... TO THE ... APOCA- ... E CAN ... MON!

BE GRATEFUL THAT THE CENTURIES HAVE TAUGHT ME NOT TO WASTE WHAT MIGHT PROVE USEFUL!

THE ORDER THAT PRESERVES *MICHAEL'S* LIFE KEEPS *YOU* ALIVE, AS WELL!

BUT DO NOT BALK ME *AGAIN,* FRENZY, FOR EVEN *APOCA-LYPSE'S* PATIENCE HAS ITS LIMITS!

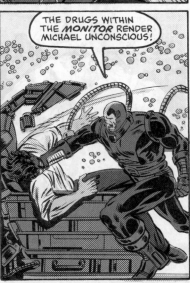

THE DRUGS WITHIN THE *MONITOR* RENDER MICHAEL UNCONSCIOUS!

NOW, HIS ... SURGE ... S TO FADE! ... RETURN TO ... ORATORY ... TO TEST ... RTHER!

FLAWED THOUGH YOU ARE, ALLIANCE, KNOW THAT APOCALYPSE IS PLEASED WITH YOU, FOR IN YOUR RUSH TO DESTROY, YOU FURTHER MY GOALS!

MUTANT *MUST* FIGHT MUTANT, IF THE WEAK ARE TO BE WINNOWED FROM THE *STRONG!*

AND WHEN ONLY THE STRONG ARE LEFT, *APOCA-LYPSE* WILL MAKE HIS MOVE!

PRAY, *ALL* OF YOU, THAT YOU ARE AMONG THE *STRONG!*

AND WITH THE WHIRL OF MACHINERY, APOCALYPSE'S PLATFORM *RETURNS* TO HIS LABORATORY BELOW.

THAT EVENING...

AS I FLEW STINGER'S BLA BLEW OUT T ROOF--OVE *THERE!*

I DIDN'T SE HIM, BUT MIK INSIDE SOME WHERE--I KNOW IT!

SO LET'S GO GET HIM *BACK!*

IT'S NOT LIKE WE HAVE A *CHOICE!* THAT JUNKIE *KNOWS* WHO WE ARE!

ANGEL, YOU AND JEAN RECONNOITER THROUGH THE HOLE IN THE ROOF! BEAST, CHECK THE WINDOWS!

ICEMAN AND I WILL WAIT FOR YOU HERE!

READY, MATA HARI?

WHE YOU OC

IT'S REALLY NICE UP HERE, ISN'T IT, SCOTT?

IT REMINDS ME OF ALASKA IN THE SUMMER, WHERE MADDIE AND I AND THE BABY LIVE...*LIVED!*

SCOTT, KEEPING YOUR MARRIAGE A SECRET FROM JEAN...IT'S TEAR-ING HER APART! AND *YOU...* HAVE YOU CALLED *MADDIE?*

THERE'S NO *ANSWER,* BOBBY! I...I THINK SHE'S LEFT ME!

PART OF ME WANTS TO *FIND* HER... *EXPLAIN* ABOUT JEAN'S RESURRECTION --WHY I *HAD* TO GO TO HER...MAKE HER *FORGIVE* ME...LET ME *COME HOME!*

BUT *JEAN'S* BACK IN MY LIFE NOW, HIGH ON X-FACTOR'S PROMISE, EAGER TO RESCUE A LOVE-SICK JUNKIE LOSER...

...FLYING IN WARREN'S ARMS, TALKING TO HIM ...LAUGHING...

...AND PART OF ME WANTS TO *PUNCH* THEIR *HEARTS* OUT!

I THINK I MUST BE GOING *MAD!*

...E...R...

HE SACRIFICED HIM-SELF FOR THE WOMAN HE LOVED WHILE I CAN'T DECIDE WHO I LOVE SO I'M SACRIFICING *THEM*, INSTEAD!

MAYBE *WE'RE* THE LOSERS! WE'RE SURE NOT *PROFESSOR X!*

HOW CAN WE EXPECT TO DO ANYTHING BUT TRAIN LOSERS?

WHILE UP ABOVE...

WHAT A *MESS!* I'LL TELE-KINETICALLY CLEAR A GOOD SIZED HOLE!

THEN AWAY WE'LL GO!

WARREN, EARLIER YOU SAID "WITH ALL I *WAS* TO SCOTT?" WHAT DID YOU MEAN...*WAS?*

I WAS... ...P IN THAT ...N, SCOTT FELL ...E WITH THE ...NIX, DIDN'T ...M JUST A ...REFLEC-... ...OF HER...

...AND IT'S EATING AT HIM TILL THE VERY *SIGHT* OF ME SICKENS HIM! THAT'S *IT*, THAT *MUST* BE IT!

SO HERE'S YOUR CHANCE! SHE DESERVES TO KNOW ABOUT SCOTT'S *MARRIAGE* AND YOU WANT TO TELL HER...

...MORE THAN YOU'VE WANTED ANYTHING IN A LONG TIME! AND YET--

WHY THE SUDDEN PASSION FOR *TRUTH*, PAL? OR IS YOUR PASSION FOR SOMETHING ELSE?

JEAN...YOU'RE SELLING YOURSELF WAY *SHORT*... AND YOU'VE GOT IT ALL *WRONG!*

IT ISN'T PHOENIX! IT...IT...

THAT'S REAL *ROMANTIC*...

...BUT THIS AIN'T THE *TIME* FER IT, FER *SURE*!

THE ALLIANCE!

STINGE SMART MO WARNED M TIME TO DE HER BLA WARRE

NE THER BE ING BE

NO WONDER SCOTT MISSES *PHOENIX*! NO WONDER HE FINDS ME SO USELESS!

WHILE DOWN *BELOW,* THE BEAST CHECKS OUT THE WINDOWS...

THAT'S A *LABORATORY* INSIDE...I'M CERTAIN OF IT!

AND.. SOUNDS SOMEC SOBB

CYCLOPS-- IN *HERE!* I BELIEVE I'VE FOUND--

CYKE?

WELL, WELL! IT LOOKS AS THOUGH THE ACTION'S STARTED! I'D BEST RUSH TO THEIR AID...

...AND SINCE THE INTRUDER ALARMS HAVE ALREADY *SOUNDED, THIS* SEEMS AS FAST A ROUTE AS ANY...

CRAS

ONE WILL RE SOME T OF INTE ALONG WAY

MIKE!

EEEEE

NO! KEEP AWAY FROM US! HAVEN'T YOU HURT US ENOUGH?

HUSH! NO! I'M A FRIEND! I'VE COME TO RESCUE YOU BOTH!

BEAST! I--IT'S OKAY, SUZY! HE IS A FRIEND!

GIVE ME A MOMENT TO UNRAVEL THE COMPLEXITIES OF THAT MACHINE, MIKE! I'LL HAVE YOU FREE IN--

...DON'T! YOU'RE [WAS]TING TIME! TAKE [SUZ]Y AND LEAVE! HURRY!

[T]HIS MACHINE... IT [M]ONITORS MY BLOOD, [S]UPPLIES ME WITH HEROIN, [T]HEN BLOCKS MY ABILITY [T]O ABSORB IT WHEN I'M... NEEDED!

GO! I--I'M NOT WORTH SAVING!

YOU UNDER-RATE YOURSELF, MICHAEL! AS A MUTANT, YOU OUT-VALUE ANY HUMAN ALIVE!

YOUR ATTACHMENT TO THE GIRL DOES YOU LITTLE CREDIT, MICHAEL! IT WEAKENS YOU!

PERHAPS THE TIME HAS COME TO REMOVE THAT WEAKNESS, SO THAT YOU CAN BE MADE STRONG!

YOU AND WHAT ARMY?

YOW! HIS ARMS! THEY'VE BECOME HAMMERS! STRETCHING IN FRONT OF ME-- SO FAST, I--

DEFEAT BY APOCALYPSE IS NO SHAME, MUTANT...

UGH!

SLAM!

--FOR AGAINST APOCALYPSE EVEN THE STRONG MUST FALL!

MEANWHILE, ICEMAN'S ICE SLIDE SKIMS OVER THE RIM OF THE BLASTED ROOF AND...

HERE'S WHERE I GET OFF, ICEMAN! THANKS FOR THE RIDE!

FRENZY! MORE OF THEM!

STOP THEM, FOOLS! STINGER AND I WILL TAKE CARE OF THE GIRL!

YOUR WISH IS MY COMMAND, FRENZY! NOW I'M HERE...

...AND NOW I'M THERE! CATCH ME IF YOU CAN--

UGH!

OOF!

MARVEL GIRL! FRENZY'S BEHIND YOU WATCH OUT!

SILLY BOY TRIED THIS BEFORE!

...WITH THE SAME APPALLING LACK OF SUCCESS!

THIS TIME I WILL GRIND YOU INTO A SNOW CONE FOR YOUR IMPERTINENCE!

NOT BAD, MARVEL GIRL! BUT NOT SO MARVELOUS, EITHER!

MY BOLTS CAN'T GET IN, BUT YOU CAN'T GET OUT! YOU'RE NO HELP TO ANYBODY!

TOWER, GRAB THAT WINGED ANGEL--HE CAN'T BE THAT FAST--AN' I'LL SHOW HER WHAT I MEAN, FER SURE!

FOR NOW, *YOU* ARE THE *STRONG*... BUT HEED ME WELL! IT WASN'T THE DRUGS, BUT MICHAEL'S WEAKNESS FOR A *HUMAN*, THAT DESTROYED HIM!

A SIMILAR WEAKNESS COULD DESTROY YOU ALL!

AND NOW I BID YOU ALL *ADIEU!* DO NOT TRY TO FIND ME!

A SEARCH WOULD PROVE FRUITLESS, SO MANY AND VARIED ARE MY GUISES!

HEY! THE BOSS *CUT OUT!* LET'S *SPLIT!*

H C T WE TUR BUM

FA

BUT NO! THEY'RE *STILL* MUTANTS LIKE US-- WE *CAN'T* TURN THEM OVER TO OUR GREATEST ENEMIES! NO MATTER WHAT.

WEEEE000EEE

HEY! LOOK! MUTIES!

NAB 'EM!

WHAT'S THAT STUFF ON THE HOUSE?

ICE, LIK AT THE M THESE GO BE THE M WHO HOL UP THER

WHAT'S *WITH* YOU, ANGEL? ARE YOU *NUTS?*

JUST TAKING OUT SOME IN- SURANCE THAT THE ALLIANCE "KNOWS" WE AREN'T *X-FACTOR!*

THEY,...GUESSED THERE WAS A CONNECTION... BUT I *NEVER* TOLD...NO MATTER WHAT!

I KNEW THAT, MIKE... WE *ALL* KNEW, DIDN'T WE, SCOTT?

SUZY'S *DEAD,* ISN'T SHE? I... I *KNEW* THEY'D KILL HER...*I'D* KILL HER...

IT WAS ACCIDE MIKE! CAN'T B YOURS

KE YOU TO OUR
QUARTERS, CREATE
G TO ENABLE
CONTROL
R POWER--

AREN'T
SWER,
I WAS A
BEFORE
A MUTANT!
N'T EVEN
RMAL
FE!

BETTER
Y...FOR
T WHAT
E DOING...
GOOD!

HERE'RE
ERS WHO
ED...WHO
ERVE...
UR HELP!
LP THEM...

THERE'S OUR ANSWER,
SCOTT! MAYBE WE'RE
NOT PROFESSOR X!
PROBABLY WE'LL
NEVER BE AS
GOOD!

BUT XAVIER'S
GONE AND
WE'RE ALL
THEY HAVE
LEFT!

I GUESS
ROTTEN
THINGS
HAPPEN TO
EVERYBODY!

MAYBE...IT
DOESN'T REALLY
MATTER WHAT
HAPPENS....IT'S
HOW WE HANDLE
THEM THAT'S THE
MEASURE OF
OUR WORTH!

G AT
AND
E HANDLED
OBLEMS
RETTY
L!

DIDN'T
THE OTHERS
EE JEAN
THE FIGHT?
IDN'T THEY
NDERSTAND?

COME ON, JEANIE,
WE'D BETTER GO!
THE POLICE WON'T
MILL AROUND OUT
THERE FOREVER!

THERE WAS FLAME AROUND
HER-- BIRD SHAPED! BUT
THE PHOENIX EFFECT?

PHOENIX IS DEAD!
I SAW HER DIE!
BUT THEN...WE
THOUGHT JEAN
WAS DEAD, TOO!

IS IT POSSIBLE? CAN
PHOENIX HAVE SURVIVED?
CAN JEAN AND PHOENIX
REALLY BE ONE?

NEXT
ISSUE: **FALL OUT**

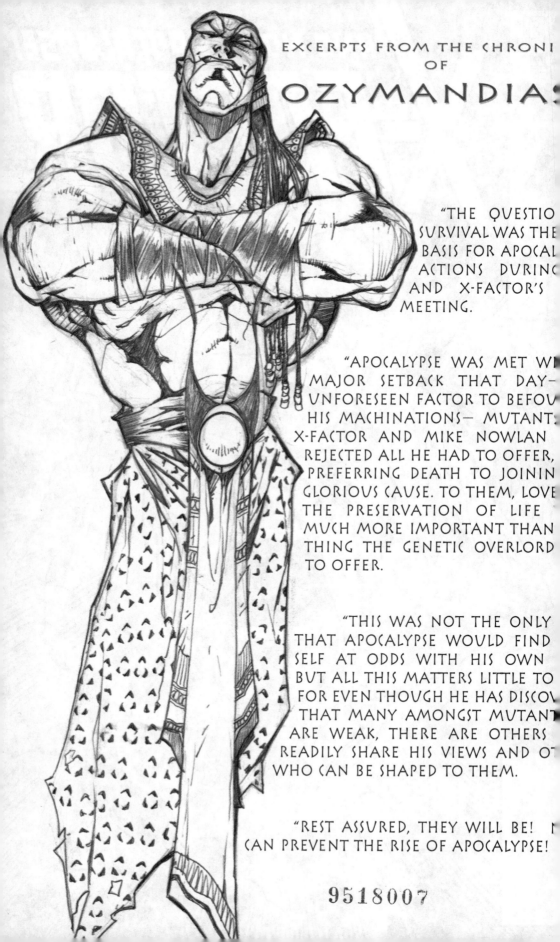

EXCERPTS FROM THE CHRONI
OF

OZYMANDIA:

"THE QUESTIO
SURVIVAL WAS THE
BASIS FOR APOCAL
ACTIONS DURINC
AND X-FACTOR'S
MEETING.

"APOCALYPSE WAS MET WI
MAJOR SETBACK THAT DAY—
UNFORESEEN FACTOR TO BEFOU
HIS MACHINATIONS— MUTANT:
X-FACTOR AND MIKE NOWLAN
REJECTED ALL HE HAD TO OFFER,
PREFERRING DEATH TO JOININ
GLORIOUS CAUSE. TO THEM, LOVE
THE PRESERVATION OF LIFE
MUCH MORE IMPORTANT THAN
THING THE GENETIC OVERLORD
TO OFFER.

"THIS WAS NOT THE ONLY
THAT APOCALYPSE WOULD FIND
SELF AT ODDS WITH HIS OWN
BUT ALL THIS MATTERS LITTLE TO
FOR EVEN THOUGH HE HAS DISCOV
THAT MANY AMONGST MUTANT
ARE WEAK, THERE ARE OTHERS
READILY SHARE HIS VIEWS AND OT
WHO CAN BE SHAPED TO THEM.

"REST ASSURED, THEY WILL BE!
CAN PREVENT THE RISE OF APOCALYPSE!

9518007